DRONFIELD HENRY FANSHAWE SCHOOL.

000013

Book No. 49

This book is the property of the Governors of the School. It must always be neatly covered. It must never be marked in any way.

NAME	Form	Date of Issue	Teacher's Initials
Elizabeth Wise	B.Wm		

THE ALFRETON COOKERY BOOK

The Alfreton Cookery Book

**By Gillian Crompton
Mair Boothby
and Jean Smith**

with drawings by Eileen Poston

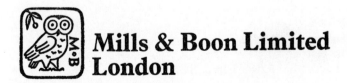

**Mills & Boon Limited
London**

First published
1971 by Mills & Boon Limited
17-19 Foley Street, London W1A 1DR

© Gillian Crompton, Mair Boothby and Jean Smith 1972
ISBN 0.263.51662.8

© illustrations—Mills & Boon 1972

Made and printed in Great Britain by
The Garden City Press Limited
Letchworth, Hertfordshire, SG6 1JS

Contents

Authors' note

The main aim of this book, founded on our collective teaching experience, is to give the reader what is needed to approach O Level or CSE examinations with confidence

While we hope we have put in dishes that are interesting and rewarding to make, we have felt bound to exclude those that are too ambitious, making excessive demands on skill or resources. So often one sees it happen that after a demonstration lesson, girls go eagerly to the bookshelves and select a recipe that is more difficult than they realise, or that calls for some rare or expensive ingredient. The teacher has to steer them towards some other choice, and this causes disappointment and frustration. In this book, we believe, a girl who has been shown a given method can try any recipe relating to it, with a good chance of success.

The book can, of course, be used selectively. For instance, we have often preferred margarine to butter as a fat, not simply for cheapness (though this is a consideration) but because certain margarines really are easier to cream than butter. Also, margarine has a nutritional value of its own. Some users of the book, however, will prefer to make a different choice. It seems sensible to leave this as taken for granted, rather than ponderously to list all the alternatives every time.

All the recipes have been repeatedly tested, and the 25 g basic unit is the same as that recommended by the Working Party of the UK Federation for Education in Home Economics. Oven temperatures have been left in degrees F, as we understand that cookers marked in degrees C will not be available for some considerable time yet. However, a conversion table is provided.

We should like to express our warm thanks to the Headmaster of Mortimer Wilson Comprehensive School, Alfreton, Derbyshire, for giving us freedom to experiment with cookery lessons in metric terms, and to the girls who worked so enthusiastically with the 'new' measures.

G. C.   M. B.   J. S.

1
Temperatures

Electric cooker manufacturers have agreed degree Celsius scale markings for oven thermostats. These will probably be introduced in 1973. The main divisions will be at 50°C intervals, with intermediate marks at 10°C. The proposed table of temperature equivalents is as follows:

° Centigrade	° Fahrenheit	Gas mark	Description
70°C	150°F		
80°C	175°F		
100°C	200°F	$\frac{1}{4}$	
110°C	225°F	$\frac{1}{2}$	very slow
130°C	250°F	$\frac{3}{4}$	
140°C	275°F	1	slow
150°C	300°F	2	moderately
170°C	325°F	3	slow
180°C	350°F	4	moderate
190°C	375°F	5	moderately
200°C	400°F	6	hot
220°C	425°F	7	hot
230°C	450°F	8	very hot
240°C	475°F	9	

Frying temperatures

°F	°C
300°F	150°C
340°F	170°C
350°F	175°C
300°F	180°C
370°F	190°C
380°F	195°C
390°F	200°C

2
Catering helpings

Average portions are given. The amount served depends upon the needs of the person eating the meal, the kind of meal served, the cost of the meal and the season of the year.

Raw weight servings are given.

Fruit juice	115 *ml*
Soup	200 *ml*
Hors d'oeuvre	110 *g*
Fish	100 *g (off the bone)*
Meat	125 *g (off the bone)*
Meat	150 *g (on the bone)*
Cheese	75 *g*
Eggs	100 *g (2 eggs)*
Vegetables	100 *g (more if there is a large amount of wastage and less if two vegetables plus potatoes are served).*
Potatoes	200 *g*
Gravy	30 *ml*
Milk Puddings	150 *ml (milk)*
Cold Sweets	125–150 *g*
Fruit	100 *g*
Pastries and puddings, using flour	25–45 *g*
Sweet sauce	50 *ml*
Beverages	200 *ml (approx).*

3

Basic recipes

Soups

Purée
1 litre stock
25 g flour
25 g fat
750 g fresh vegetables or
175 g pulse vegetables
250 g flavouring vegetables
Bouquet garni
Seasonings

Broth
1 litre beef stock
150 g meat
250 g vegetables (carrots, turnip,
swede, leek, onion, celery)
25 g barley
Bouquet garni
Seasoning

Sauces

Roux

Pouring
25 g fat
25 g flour
500 ml milk

Coating
50 g fat
50 g flour
500 ml milk

Panada
100 g fat
100 g flour
500 ml milk

Blending

Pouring
25 g powder
(cornflour, custard powder)
25 g sugar if a sweet sauce
500 ml milk

Jam sauce	500 ml liquid (consisting of jam, fruit juices, etc.) 25 g arrowroot or cornflour Sugar to taste

Milk puddings

Whole grain (Rice)	500 ml milk 50 g rice Pinch salt Knob of margarine 50 g sugar
Medium grain (Sago, tapioca)	500 ml milk 50 g sugar 50 g grain
Ground grain (Ground rice, semolina)	500 ml milk 50 g grain 50 g sugar
Baked egg custard	500 ml milk 2–3 eggs 50 g sugar

Suet sponge puddings

Steamed	250 g S.R. flour 100 g suet 100 g sugar 125 ml milk 1 egg

Batters

Pancake (Pouring)	125 ml milk 1 egg 100 g plain flour (strong) $\frac{1}{4}$ teasp. salt
Coating (1) Fritter	1 egg white 50 g plain flour Pinch salt 3–4 tablesp. water 2 teasp. olive oil

| (2) Economical for Fish | 50 g S.R. flour
Pinch salt
4 tablesp. water |

Pastry

Shortcrust	200 g flour 50 g margarine $\frac{1}{2}$ level teasp. salt 50 g lard 8–10 teasp. water
Rough puff/flaky	200 g plain strong flour 75 g lard 75 g margarine $\frac{1}{2}$ level teasp. salt 125 ml water Few drops lemon juice or pinch of cream of tartar
Suet	250 g S.R. flour 100–125 g suet $\frac{1}{2}$ level teasp. salt 125 ml water (approx.)

Cakes

Plain (Rubbed in)	200 g flour 100 g margarine 100 g sugar 2 level teasp baking powder 2 eggs
Rich (Creamed)	100 g flour 100 g margarine 100 g caster sugar 2 eggs $\frac{1}{4}$ teasp. baking powder or less Up to double quantity of flour may be used
Sponges (Whisked)	50 g caster sugar 2 eggs 50 g flour
Gingerbread	To 250 g flour 100–125 g fat 100–125 g sugar 120–150 g syrup 0–1 eggs

Scones

½ level teasp. raising agent, bicarbonate
of soda
1 level teasp. ginger
Spice (optional)
125 ml liquid
250 g flour
125 ml milk (approx.) or 1 egg + 4
tablesp. milk
25–50 g margarine
25–50 g sugar if used
1 level teasp. salt
4 level teasp. baking powder
100 g cheese ⎱
50 g fruit   ⎰
(optional—for variations)

Bread

Plain
500 g plain strong flour
15 g yeast
1 round teasp. salt
300 ml water
1 round teasp. sugar

Rich
500 g plain strong flour
15 g yeast
1 round teasp. sugar
25–50 g fat
1 round teasp. salt
300 ml water and milk mixed

NOTE: Spoon measures, other than for liquids, are rounded
throughout this book unless level measures are specified.

4

Cookery terms

à la carte	Dishes prepared to order and priced individually.
à la française	In the French style.
Aspic	Savoury jelly used for decorative work.
Au gratin	Sprinkled with cheese and/or bread crumbs and browned under the grill or in the oven.
Bain-marie	Water bath. A container of water in which dishes are placed in the oven to prevent overcooking, e.g. custard. The water must not boil.
Bake blind	To line a flan ring with pastry, prick and weigh down with greaseproof paper and baking beans or rice or with foil to keep in shape during cooking. The paper, etc., is removed 5 mins. before cooking is completed. The filling is added when the pastry is cool.
Bard	To cover the breasts of poultry with fat bacon.
Baste	To pour hot fat over foods to keep them moist while cooking.
Blanch	(a) To whiten or remove strong flavour by bringing foods to the boil in water, then refreshing in cold. Used for celery, onions, green peppers, etc. (b) To remove the skin from nuts and tomatoes. Nuts are immersed in cold water, brought to the boil, refreshed in cold and the skins removed. Tomatoes: Boil some water. Remove from the heat. Immerse tomatoes in water 2 mins. Refresh in cold, remove skins.
Blend	To mix together a solid and a liquid ingredient, as in custard.

Bouquet garni	(B.G.) A sprig of parsley, piece of thyme and a bayleaf tied in muslin. Used for flavouring soups, stews and casseroles.
Casserole	A fire-proof dish with a lid, also refers to a mixture of meat or vegetables cooked in a covered dish in the oven and served in that same dish.
Consommé	A clear soup.
Croquettes	Cooked foods, e.g. potato, moulded into a cylinder shape, egged, crumbed and deep fried.
Croûte	A large piece of fried bread or toast on which savouries are served.
Croûtons	Cubes of fried bread or toast served with soup.
Dariole	A small mould used for castle puddings, etc.
Doyley	A fancy paper used in serving sweet dishes.
Dish paper	A plain paper used in serving savoury dishes.
Dice, to	Cut into small even-sized pieces.
Flan	An open tart.
Fricassée	A white stew, meat or poultry cooked in a sauce.
Garnish, to	To decorate a savoury dish with parsley, lemon, mushroom, tomato, hard boiled eggs, etc.
Gâteau	A fancy cake of more than one portion.
Glaze, to	To brush over the tops of pies, buns, etc., to improve the appearance. Egg wash or sugar and water may be used. Flan glaze is made from fruit juice and arrowroot cooked to a clear gel.
Hors d'oeuvre	Small portions of meat, fish or vegetables served as a first course.
Liaison	A thickening.
Mirepoix	A bed of diced root vegetables on which meat and vegetables are placed for braising.
Maître d'hôtel butter	Butter containing lemon juice and chopped parsley, used for serving with grilled meats.
Panada	A very thick sauce made from flour, fat and liquid, used for binding.
Prove, to	To allow a yeast dough to rest in a warm place so it can rise and expand.
Pulses	Vegetables grown in pods, e.g. peas, beans, lentils.

Purée	A smooth pulp obtained by sieving.
Raspings	Golden bread crumbs used for coating foods to be fried.
Refresh, to	To place in cold water to cool.
Réchauffer	To re-heat.
Roux	A thickening of fat and flour used in sauces.
Seasoned flour	Plain flour mixed with salt and pepper.
Sweat, to	To cook in fat in a closed pan without colouring but making more tender.
Sauté	(a) Tossed in fat; (b) Cooked quickly in a frying pan.
Soufflé	A very light dish, sweet or savoury, hot or cold.
Stock	Water in which meat and/or vegetables have been cooked; used for soup, gravies, sauces.
Table d'hôte	A meal at a fixed price.
Vol-au-vent	A large puff pastry case.
Zest	The coloured part of orange or lemon skin which contains the flavouring oils.

5

Hors d'oeuvre and first courses

(See also Salads and Beverages)

GRAPEFRUIT (Orange may be prepared in the same way)

1 Cut across in half.
2 Loosen each segment from its enclosing skin with a grapefruit knife.
3 Sprinkle with sugar. Decorate with half a glacé cherry.

Preparation of grapefruit

GRAPEFRUIT AND ORANGE COCKTAIL

Allow half orange and half grapefruit per head.

1 Cut into half and remove segments from fruit.
2 Mix together lightly with sugar. Pile back into grapefruit skin or glass dish. Decorate with half a glacé cherry.

N.B. Fruit edges may be cut in a zig-zag using a sharp pointed knife.

GRILLED GRAPEFRUIT

To each half fruit:
15 g butter   *1 teasp. Barbados sugar*

1 Halve the grapefruit, loosen segments.
2 Dot with butter, sprinkle with sugar.
3 Grill until sugar and butter caramelise (golden brown).
4 Serve in a grapefruit dish.

MINT GRAPEFRUIT

Grapefruit
Peppermint creams   *Fresh mint*

1 Halve and segment fruit, chop peppermint creams, sprinkle on top.
2 Garnish with fresh mint.

MELON

Approx. half melon for 3–4 portions, depending on size.

1 Cut melon in half, remove pips, cut into 4 portions lengthways.
2 Loosen flesh from skin, using a sharp knife. Cut into equal cubes.
3 Decorate with cherries or slices of lemon or orange on cocktail sticks.
   Serve with ginger and caster sugar.

SHELLFISH COCKTAIL

Half lettuce
125 g–175 g prepared prawns   *Lemon slices for garnish*
or shrimps

Sauce:
5 tablesp. home-made or   *Seasoning*
bought mayonnaise or lightly   *Few drops of lemon juice*
whipped cream   *1 tablesp. sherry (optional)*

3 tablesp. tomato ketchup or
purée

1 Mix all sauce ingredients together; taste and adjust seasoning.
2 Wash, dry and shred the lettuce finely. Place in glasses or in shell dishes.
3 Mix shellfish with sauce, leaving some for garnish. Pile on to lettuce.
4 Garnish with slices of lemon. Stand each dish on a small plate.

STUFFED EGGS

2 eggs   Seasoning
2 tablesp. mayonnaise

Filling:
25 g cheese or 1 blanched   Cream cheese may be used
tomato or 2 sardines or 1 tab-   without mayonnaise.
lesp. chopped chives.
Parsley or cayenne pepper for garnish.

1 Hard boil 2 eggs, 10 mins.; cool. Shell.
2 Cut in half lengthwise, remove yolks with a teaspoon and sieve into a basin.
3 Add mayonnaise, seasoning, and flavouring (grate cheese finely, chop sardines, chives, sieve tomato). The consistency should be that of whipped cream. If necessary add more mayonnaise.
4 Pipe with a star savoy tube or pile into the whites.
5 Garnish with parsley or sprinkle with cayenne pepper. Serve on an oval plate with a dish paper.

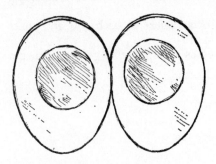

Eggs cut lengthways for stuffed eggs and salads

EGG MAYONNAISE

2 hard boiled eggs.   *Tomato or anchovy strips or*
Lettuce.   *parsley or capers for garnish*
Mayonnaise

1 Hard boil eggs, 10 mins. Cool and shell.
2 Cut into half lengthwise or slice. Place each on a lettuce leaf in a small dish. Coat with mayonnaise. Garnish.

CREAM CHEESE BALLS

Cream cheese and a combination of chopped nuts, chopped chives, grated cheese, chopped cucumber, chopped dates, chopped parsley, seasoning, golden breadcrumbs or nuts for rolling.

1 Beat the cream cheese till smooth. Add chosen flavouring to make a stiff consistency. Season.
2 Roll into balls, coat in chopped nuts or breadcrumbs. Serve in a small dish.

CORN ON THE COB

1 cob, fresh or frozen, per person.
To choose fresh, pull away leaves and silk from the top to see if the cob is full to the top with corn; this should be small and fine, not coarse, or the corn will be tough.

1 Remove silk and leaves by pulling together from the top. Remove end stalk and wash.
2 Cook in boiling water, unsalted, 20 mins. till tender. (Salt makes the corn tough.) Do not overcook or toughening occurs.
3 Strain, serve with cocktail sticks in each end and cover with melted butter and salt.

N.B. Corn may be served as a dessert with golden or maple syrup.

STUFFED TOMATOES

4 firm tomatoes   *Seasoning*
Filling:
    e.g. 50 g grated cheese or $\frac{1}{2}$ pkt. cream cheese, and chopped nuts; or cottage cheese and chives; or chopped ham; or

chopped celery; or chopped hard boiled eggs; or chopped sardines; or cooked rice and mushrooms; or shrimps etc.

Garnish:
Watercress or parsley

1 Wash tomatoes, remove stalks. Stand tomato on stalk end and cut a thin slice off the opposite end.
2 Scoop out the flesh with a teaspoon and sieve. Mix with the chosen filling and seasoning.
3 Pile back into tomato. Replace the lid.
4 Serve on an oval dish, garnish with watercress or parsley.

N.B. For hot stuffed tomatoes see the section on vegetables.

6

Soups

MEAT STOCK

Raw or cooked bones, skin and gristle of meat or poultry or poultry giblets
Cold water to cover bones
Onion
Carrot
Celery (optional)
Use only fresh or freshly cooked ingredients.

Remove any fat. Place all in a pan. Cover. Simmer 2–3 hours. Strain. If kept boil each day.

FISH STOCK

Fish bones and white skin
Cold water
Sliced onion

Place in a pan. Simmer 20 mins. Strain.

SCOTCH BROTH

25 g pearl barley
200 g scrag end neck of mutton
1½ litres beef stock or water
Up to 250 g mixed vegetables (carrot, turnip, swede, leek, celery, onion, diced very small)

Seasoning
2 teasp. chopped parsley

1 Wash barley. Remove fat from meat. Cut into pieces.
2 Put meat and stock in a saucepan. Soak 15 mins.
3 Cook slowly 1 hour. Skim off fat.
4 Add vegetables and seasoning. Simmer 1 hour, skimming occasionally. Remove meat.

5 Dice about two tablesp. of the meat. Return to pan.
6 Reheat, taste, re-season if necessary, skim.
7 Serve in a tureen, sprinkled with chopped parsley.

LENTIL SOUP

150–200 g lentils (dry weight)	*Seasoning*
1 litre stock or water	*Bouquet garni*
1 small carrot	*25 g margarine*
1 onion	*25 g plain flour*
1 stick of celery	*125 ml milk*
	Croûtons for garnish

1 Wash lentils, place in a saucepan with stock or water.
2 Shred the carrot, slice the onion and celery and add to the pan.
3 Add seasonings, simmer 1½–2 hrs.
4 Rub through a sieve. Melt fat in the saucepan. Add the flour, mix well and stir in the milk slowly to make a roux sauce. Then add the sieved soup. Season.
5 Boil 4–5 mins. stirring. Taste. Re-season if necessary.
6 Serve in a tureen with croûtons.

PEA SOUP

250 g dried peas	*Bouquet garni*
1 litre water	*25 g margarine*
½ small swede	*25 g flour*
2 sticks celery	*125 ml milk*
Seasoning	*A ham bone if possible*

1 Wash peas, soak overnight, in cold water (use the water for the soup).
2 Make as for lentil soup, adding the ham bone and swede at point 2.

POTATO SOUP

500 g potatoes	*Seasoning*
Small onion	*2 cloves*
1 stick celery	*1 blade mace*
25 g margarine	*250 ml milk*
1 litre white stock or water	*Parsley and croûtons for garnish*

1 Peel and cut potatoes, onion, celery into thin slices.
2 Melt the fat, sweat the vegetables with a lid on the pan for 10–15 mins., till all the fat is absorbed.
3 Add stock and seasonings, simmer 1 hour.
4 Sieve, reboil. Add milk. Boil 10 mins. stirring. Taste and re-season if necessary.
5 Serve in a tureen with chopped parsley sprinkled on top and with croûtons.

TOMATO SOUP

500 g tomatoes, fresh or canned   Bouquet garni
1 onion   Seasoning
1 carrot   Sugar to taste
Bacon rinds   125 ml milk
25 g margarine   Parsley,   croûtons   or
25 g cornflour   Parmesan cheese for garnish
1 litre stock or water

1 Wash tomatoes, slice. If canned, remove juice, use as part of the stock.
2 Grate the carrot, slice the onion. Put bacon rind and margarine into a pan. Add vegetables when the fat has melted.
3 Place a lid on the pan. Sweat 10–15 mins., shake occasionally.
4 Add the stock and seasoning. Simmer 1–1½ hrs. Rub through a sieve. Blend the milk and cornflour together. Add this to the sieved soup. Return to the pan. Boil 3–4 mins., stirring.
5 Taste and add sugar if necessary.
6 Serve in a tureen with chopped parsley sprinkled on top. Croûtons or grated Parmesan cheese may be offered.

CELERY SOUP

1 head celery (approx. 500 g)   Bouquet garni
1 onion   Seasoning
25 g margarine   25 g cornflour
1 litre white stock   Croûtons for garnish
125 ml milk

1 Slice celery and onion thinly. Melt the fat in a saucepan. Sweat the vegetables 10–15 mins., with a lid on the pan. Shake occasionally.
2 Add stock and seasonings. Simmer 1–1½ hrs., till vegetables are tender. Sieve.
3 Blend the milk and cornflour; add to the sieved soup.
4 Return soup to the rinsed pan. Boil 3–4 mins., stirring. Taste. Re-season if necessary.
5 Serve in a tureen with croûtons.

SEASONAL VEGETABLE SOUP

500 g mixed vegetables (onion, carrot, swede, leek or chives, celery, mushrooms, tomato (skinned), parsnip, turnip) 25 g margarine

1 litre stock Bouquet garni Seasoning 25 g cornflour Rolls to serve or croûtons for garnish

1 Prepare and dice the vegetables.
2 Melt the margarine in a saucepan. Sweat vegetables 10–15 mins.
3 Add stock and seasonings. Simmer 45–60 mins., till vegetables are tender. Remove bouquet garni.
4 Blend cornflour with a little cold water. Add a little of the hot liquid from the pan. Pour into the soup, stirring. Boil 3–4 mins. Taste, re-season if necessary.
5 Serve in a tureen with rolls or croûtons.

ONION SOUP (brown or white)

1 kilo onions 25 g margarine 15 g flour

1½ litres brown or white stock Seasoning 50 g grated cheese

1 Peel onions and slice thinly.
2 Melt butter in a pan. Add onion. Sauté until the onion is tender and golden for a brown soup. Sweat with a lid on the pan, 20–30 mins. till tender for white soup. Do not colour.
3 Mix in the flour, cook over a moderate heat, browning slightly for a brown soup.
4 Gradually mix in the stock. Bring to the boil, skim and season. Simmer about 10 mins. till the onion is soft.

5 Taste and re-season if necessary. Serve in a tureen. Sprinkle the cheese on top and offer slices of French bread or crusty rolls.

CHICKEN BROTH

1 carrot	*1 chicken stock cube*
1 large onion	*1 litre chicken stock or water*
1 stick celery	*Bouquet garni*
50 g mushrooms	*Seasoning*
1 small boiling chicken	*50 g noodles*

1 Peel and dice the carrot and onion. Chop the celery and mushrooms.
2 Place the chicken, vegetables, crumbled stock cube and liquid into a saucepan. Add bouquet garni and seasoning.
3 Bring to the boil. Simmer for approx. 2 hrs. till the chicken is tender. Add the noodles 30 mins. before the chicken is ready. Cook until tender.
4 Remove the chicken from the pan. Take off the skin.
5 Reboil the broth, taste, re-season if necessary. Serve in a soup tureen as the first course.
6 The chicken may be served as a second course with accompanying vegetables, or used for rissoles, pasties, etc.

7

Fish

Choice of fish
1 Buy from a clean, well ventilated shop.
2 The fish should be firm to the touch, not flabby and moist.
3 Eyes, gills and any spots on the skin should be bright.
4 There should be no unpleasant smells.
5 Scales should be plentiful.
6 The tail should be straight and stiff.

Groups of fish used in cookery
White, e.g. plaice, sole, cod, halibut, hake, haddock, turbot, whiting.
Oily, e.g. eels, herring, mackerel, trout, salmon, sardine, sprats.
Shell, e.g. crab, cockles, mussels, whelks, lobster, prawns, shrimps, winkles.

Accompaniments for fish
(*a*) sauces: white, parsley, hard-boiled eggs, onion, anchovy, cheese, tomato, tartare.
(*b*) garnishes: lemon, tomato, mushroom, parsley, watercress.

GRILLED FISH

Cod steaks or fillets, plaice fillets, margarine, seasoned flour.
1 Heat the grill.
2 Wash and dry the fish. Remove the centre bone from cod steaks. For plaice, remove black skin, dust with seasoned flour.
3 Dot with margarine. Grill 4–5 mins. on each side, depending on the thickness, till the fish is tender.
4 Remove from grill. Serve on a hot oval dish. Garnish with

parsley and lemon. Maître d'hôtel butter may be used (see page 205).

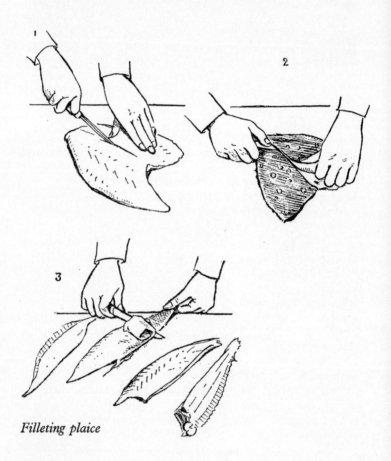

Filleting plaice

FRIED FISH

Cod steaks, or fillets, haddock or plaice fillets.

Coatings: seasoned flour, egg and raspings, or coating batter (see batters)

1 Wash, dry well, trim off any fins. Remove any skin or bones.
2 Coat with seasoned flour, egg and raspings (see Fish Cakes, p. 109) or batter.
3 Heat lard or oil in a pan till a cube of bread dropped into

it is browned in 30 secs. (Deep fat for batter, shallow for other coatings).

4 Place fish in the fat. Turn the fish in the shallow fat after 5 mins. or when the underside is golden. Fry on the second side 5 mins. Deep fry 7–10 mins. till golden. Drain.

5 Serve on a hot oval plate. Garnish with parsley or tomato or lemon.

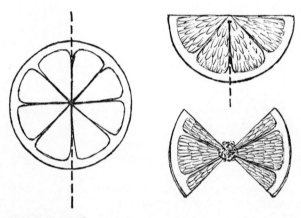

Lemon butterfly

STEAMED WHITE FISH

A whole fish or a piece of fish. Margarine, seasoning.

1 Put a large saucepan of water on to boil.

2 Wash and dry the fish. Place on a plate, add dots of margarine and seasoning. Cover with a second plate or foil. Place on the pan.

3 Steam 20–30 mins. till tender and flaky. Drain. Remove bones.

4 Serve on a hot oval plate. Garnish with lemon and parsley.

BAKED COD or other white fish

500 g cod   *Seasoning*
250 ml milk   *Bay leaf*
Knob of margarine

1 Oven 350°F/Gas Mark 4. Grease a shallow casserole dish liberally with the margarine.

2 Wash, dry and skin the fish, remove any large bones. Place in the dish. Season.
3 Pour the milk over the fish. Add the bay leaf. Cover with a lid or foil.
4 Cook, middle shelf 20–30 mins. until the fish flakes.
5 Lift out the fish, place on a warm oval dish, garnish with parsley or lemon. The milk may be used to make a sauce (see sauces).

BAKED STUFFED COD

25 g margarine
4 cod steaks
50 g breadcrumbs
1 teasp. dried parsley

$\frac{1}{2}$ teasp. lemon juice or finely grated zest
Seasoning
Beaten egg or milk to bind

1 Oven 350°F/Gas Mark 4.
2 Grease a casserole dish with margarine.
3 Wash and dry fish. Remove centre bone leaving skin intact.
4 Prepare stuffing, mix all the dry ingredients and bind with beaten egg or milk to a stiff consistency.
5 Place steaks in the dish. Fill the centres with stuffing. Place a knob of margarine on each steak. Cover with foil or a lid. Bake 20–30 mins. till tender.
6 Remove skin and serve on an oval plate. Garnish with lemon and parsley. Serve with a sauce, e.g. white, cheese or parsley (see sauces p. 195).

N.B. This dish may be made using fillets of cod with stuffing between or fillets of plaice rolled round stuffing.

COD AU GRATIN

500 g cod
25 g margarine
25 g flour
250 ml milk

50 g finely grated cheese
Parsley and tomatoes for garnish
Raspings (optional)

1 Bake, steam or poach the fish.
2 Prepare a roux sauce, coating consistency (see sauces p. 197, using margarine, flour and milk), add $\frac{2}{3}$ of the cheese, season.
3 Place fish in an au gratin or shallow casserole dish. Pour over the sauce. Sprinkle remaining cheese on top. Grill till golden brown.

4 Garnish with parsley or slices of tomato.

N.B. Raspings may be sprinkled on top with the cheese.

COD PORTUGAISE

margarine
250 g cod
½ large or 1 small onion
50 g mushrooms

2 tomatoes
Raspings
50 g finely grated cheese
Seasoning

1 Oven 350°F/Gas Mark 4.
2 Liberally grease a dish with margarine.
3 Wash and dry fish. Remove bones and skin. Divide into two or three pieces.
4 Slice onion thinly and blanch in boiling water 5 mins.
5 Slice mushrooms; blanch and slice tomatoes.
6 Arrange fish, tomatoes, onion, mushrooms in layers, seasoning well.
7 Mix cheese with raspings, sprinkle on to the fish. Dot with margarine. Cover.
8 Bake from 30–40 mins. till tender.
9 Serve with a sauce, parsley or cheese as liked.

POACHED COD

500 g cod
250 ml water
Seasoning
Lemon juice

Sliced onion (optional)
Bouquet garni
Lemon or parsley for garnish

1 Wash, dry and skin fish, remove bones.
2 Place water in a shallow wide pan. Season water, add the lemon juice, onion, bouquet garni.
3 Bring water to the boil. Reduce to a simmer. Immerse fish in water. Simmer gently for 15–20 mins. till tender.
4 Remove fish, drain. Serve on a warm oval dish, garnish with lemon or parsley. The water could be strained and used with milk to make a sauce.

HERRINGS OR MACKEREL

Preparation:

1 Wash, scale by running the back of a knife from tail to head.

2 Cut off fins and remove head below gills. Leave tail on, merely trim neatly.
3 Slice down the underside (thin part) to the tail. Remove intestines and roe. Wash.
4 Place the fish skin side uppermost using the thumbs, press down on to the spine, to loosen it from the flesh. Turn fish over. Cut spine at the tail and remove from tail to head. Inspect the fish for loose bones. Remove any black skin by rubbing with salt. Wash and dry.

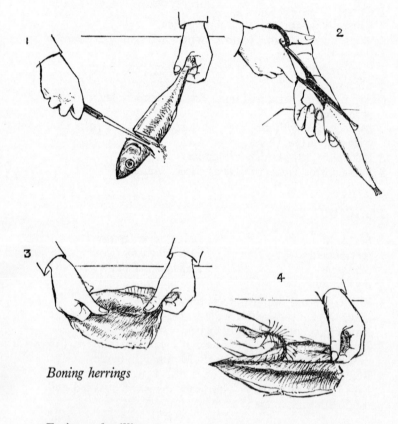

Boning herrings

Frying and grilling
Coat with seasoned flour or fine oatmeal. *Fry* open or closed in shallow fat (margarine or butter). Drain, serve on a warm oval dish, garnish with lemon or parsley.
To grill: dot with margarine, grill open turning once. Time according to size 10–15 mins. Serve as above.

Baking

Oven 350°F/Gas Mark 4. Grease a roasting tin or baking sheet with margarine. Place fish on tin with a knob of margarine and seasoning.

Bake closed for 20–30 mins., depending on size, until the thickest part is tender.

BAKED STUFFED HERRING OR MACKEREL

2 prepared herrings or mackerel
Stuffing:
50 g breadcrumbs
25 g margarine
Seasoning
1 teasp. parsley
Beaten egg to bind

extra margarine for step 5

1 Oven 350°F/Gas Mark 4. Grease a roasting tin or baking sheet with margarine.
2 Mix the stuffing ingredients to a stiff consistency with the beaten egg.
3 Spread one side of each fish with stuffing, fold over, or spread thinly all over and roll up from head to tail, tying with string.
4 Place in tin.
5 Dot with margarine. Cook 20–30 mins. till tender. Serve on an oval dish, garnish with lemon or parsley.

SOUSED HERRING OR MACKEREL

2 prepared herrings or mackerel
125 ml vinegar
125 ml water
6 peppercorns
2 cloves
Sprig of thyme

Bayleaf
2 dried chillies
1 teasp. salt
1 sliced onion may be added if liked

1 Oven 325°F/Gas Mark 3.
2 Roll up herring or mackerel from head to tail. Place in a casserole dish with the tail uppermost. Add the remaining ingredients.

3 Cover, cook 30–45 mins. till tender. Leave to cool in the liquid.
4 Serve cold with salad.

KEDGEREE

500 g fish (smoked haddock or salmon)
A tin of salmon or tuna fish may also be used
250 g patna rice
50 g margarine
Salt
Curry powder
2 hard boiled eggs
Lemon and parsley for garnish

1 Wash and dry fish, poach or steam till tender. Drain, flake, removing bones and skin.
2 Wash rice, place in boiling salted water. Boil 10–12 mins. till just cooked. Drain and pour boiling water through, drain again.
3 Melt margarine in a pan, re-heat rice and haddock by tossing in the margarine.
4 Season and add curry powder to taste.
5 Chop one egg, add to the fish. Slice the second egg for garnish.
6 Pile on an oval dish or form in a fish shape. Garnish with egg, lemon and parsley.

This dish may be served hot or cold.

8
Meat and poultry

Choice of meat
Beef: this should be dark red in colour, firm and smooth. The beef should be marbled with yellow coloured fat and should smell fresh.
Lamb: the lean should be light red in colour, fine in texture. The fat should be white and hard.
Pork: the flesh should be pale pink and the fat white and soft.

Cuts of meat to use
Roasting
Beef: sirloin, topside, thick flank, forerib.
Lamb: shoulder, leg, best end of neck, loin, breast.
Pork: leg, loin, shoulder, hand and spring, blade, spare ribs, belly.

Braising
Beef: topside, brisket, top rib, back rib, silverside.

Stewing
Beef; neck, shin, chuck steak, flank.
Lamb; scrag-end and middle neck.

Grilling and Frying
Beef; rump, fillet, sirloin steaks.
Lamb; loin chops, best end of neck cutlets.
Pork; loin chops.

Boiling
Beef; brisket, silverside, topside.
Pork: head, pieces of bacon, gammon.

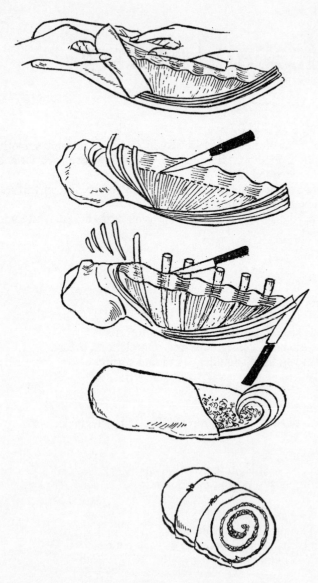

Boning, stuffing and rolling breast of lamb

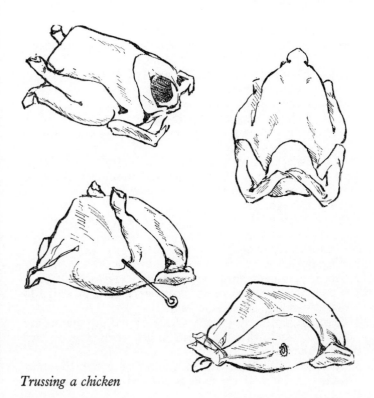

Trussing a chicken

Roasting

Temperatures 350°F/Gas Mark 4 all the time or 425°F/Gas Mark 7, 10–15 mins. reduce to 350°F/Gas Mark 4 for the majority of the cooking time, raising to 425°F/Gas Mark 7 for the last 15 mins.

Cold oven method—place the meat in a cold oven set to 400°F/Gas Mark 6. This method reduces shrinkage and can be used in time controlled ovens.

Times for roasting

As a guide only. Timing depends upon the thickness and toughness of the joint.

Beef: 15 mins. per 500 g and 15 mins. over. This gives rare meat.

Lamb: 20 mins. per 500 g and 20 mins. over.

Pork: 25 mins. per 500 g and 25 mins. over.

Ham and bacon as for pork.

Poultry: 20 mins. per 500 g and 20 mins. over.

Accompaniments for roast meat

Beef	Yorkshire pudding, horseradish sauce, or mustard. Thin dark gravy. Roast potatoes.
Lamb	Mint sauce or onion sauce or red currant jelly. Medium brown gravy.
Pork	Sage and onion stuffing. Light thick gravy. Apple sauce.
Poultry	Chipolata sausages, bacon rolls, bread sauce, thyme and parsley stuffing. Pale, slightly golden gravy.
Turkey	Can have cranberry sauce and chestnut stuffing, or as other poultry.
Duck	Orange sauce.
Ham	Pineapple and pineapple sauce or parsley sauce.

General rules for roasting
1 Wipe meat.
2 Secure in shape with string if necessary. Truss poultry.
3 Weigh the prepared joint. Score pork rind in strips to make crackling. Season the joint.
4 Place in a tin. If the joint has little fat and/or potatoes are being cooked with the meat, a little dripping or lard should be added.
5 Roast by the chosen method, basting every 15 mins. during cooking. If the joint is covered in foil, basting is not required.

Making gravy—see Sauces p. 199

Grilling

	Preparation and Method	Time
Sausage	Prick (not for skinless). Turn during cooking. Medium heat.	8–10 mins.
	Chipolata sausages.	5 mins.
Bacon	Remove rind, snip fat. Turn once during cooking. Medium heat. To crisp fat increase heat for one minute during cooking.	4–6 mins.
Lamb Chops or Cutlets	Wipe, season, brush with oil. Turn once during cooking. Medium heat.	10–15 mins
Pork Chops	Wipe, season, brush with oil. Medium heat.	15–20 mins

Steak (fillet, sirloin, rump, T-bone)	Wipe, beat to tenderise the fibres, season. Brush with oil or butter. Turn once during cooking.	Rare 5–7 mins. Medium 7–10 mins. Well done 10–15 mins
Gammon	Wipe, remove rind, any bone and excess fat. Medium heat.	5–7 mins.
Kidney	Wipe, remove skin and core, slice in half from the round side towards the core. Skewer open. Brush with oil. Turn during cooking. Medium heat.	5–6 mins.
Liver	Wash, remove blood vessels, skin and tubes. Season, brush with oil. Turn once. Low heat.	5–6 mins.

MIXED GRILL

This can include steak, chops, bacon, sausage, kidney, tomato, mushrooms.
Serve on an oval plate garnished with watercress or parsley and maître d'hôtel butter (see sauces).

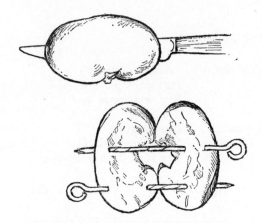

Preparation of kidneys for mixed grill

KEBABS

A collection of small pieces of meat and vegetables threaded on skewers, brushed with oil and grilled. 1 skewer per person. Each skewer may hold 1 or 2 cubes of tender steak, 1 or 2 bacon rolls, 1 or 2 button or pieces of mushroom, 1 kidney, 1 small sausage and ½—1 small tomato.

Serve on a bed of rice (see curry).

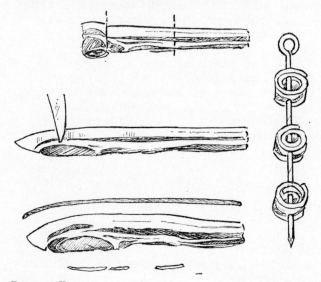

Bacon rolls

BROWN STEW (4 servings)

500 g shin or neck of beef or	*1 tomato (optional)*
chuck steak	*Parsley for garnish*
1 large onion	*25 g dripping or lard*
250 g carrots	*Seasoning*
250 g swede and/or turnip	*Bouquet garni*
150 g mushrooms (optional)	*500 ml brown stock*
1 parsnip	*25 g plain flour or cornflour*
1 stick celery	

(Amounts of different vegetables may be varied according to taste.)

1 Wipe meat. Remove excess fat and gristle. Cut into 2-centimetre cubes.

2 Dice or slice all the vegetables except the tomato.
3 Blanch the tomato, slice.
4 Melt the fat in a thick-bottomed saucepan. Fry the meat quickly till brown on all sides. Remove.
5 Add the onion and fry until the fat is absorbed.
6 Replace the meat, add the vegetables, seasoning, bouquet garni and stock.
7 Bring to the boil, cover, simmer 1½–2 hrs. till tender.
8 Make the thickening by blending the flour with cold water to a thin cream.
9 Add some of the hot liquid from the pan. Return the contents of the basin to the pan, stirring. Boil 3 mins. Remove bouquet garni, taste, re-season if necessary.
10 Serve in a casserole dish. Garnish with chopped parsley. A teasp. of vinegar or lemon juice may be added to help to tenderise the meat. This dish may be cooked in a casserole dish in the oven at 350°F/Gas Mark 4. Reduce the quantity of liquid.

For dumplings, see pastry.

N.B. A different method of thickening may be used as follows.
Add the flour after point 5, cooking till brown. Correct consistency when cooking is completed.

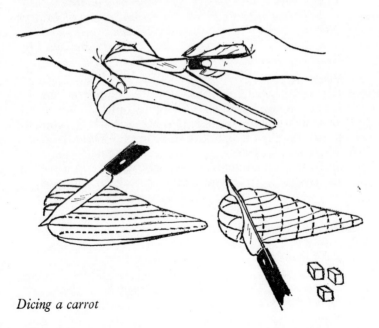

Dicing a carrot

IRISH STEW

600 g neck of lamb	*Parsley for garnish*
250 g onions	*Seasoning*
100 g celery (optional)	*500 ml white stock or water*
500 g potatoes	*Bouquet garni*

1 Wipe meat, trim off excess fat and gristle. Cut into equal sized portions leaving the bone intact.
2 Prepare vegetables, slice or dice, cut potatoes into $\frac{1}{4}$ or $\frac{1}{8}$ according to size. (Small whole new potatoes may be used.)
3 Place meat, vegetables, except potatoes, seasoning, stock and bouquet garni in a pan. Bring to the boil. Cover. Simmer 1–1$\frac{1}{2}$ hrs. till tender.
4 Half an hour before the stew is ready, add the potatoes.
5 Taste, re-season if necessary. Remove bouquet garni.
6 Serve in a casserole dish, sprinkled with chopped parsley. Serve peas or green vegetables and carrots to add colour.

SAVOURY MINCE

500 g minced beef	*50 g mushrooms or 2 blanched*
1 large onion	*tomatoes may be added*
25 g dripping or lard	*25 g cornflour or plain flour*
250 ml stock	*may be added*
Seasoning	*Parsley and croûtons for*
Bouquet garni	*garnish*

1 Wash meat.
2 Dice onion. Melt fat and sweat the onion until tender.
3 Add the minced beef, cook till lightly brown.
4 Add the liquor, seasoning, other vegetables, bouquet garni; bring to the boil. Cover, simmer $\frac{1}{2}$–$\frac{3}{4}$ hr. till tender.
5 Thicken as for brown stew. Remove bouquet garni.
6 Serve in a casserole dish. Garnish with chopped parsley and croûtons. Serve with green vegetables and potatoes.

STEAK AND ONIONS

500 g chuck steak	*15 g cornflour*
2 large onions	*Parsley and grilled tomatoes*
Seasoning	*for garnish*
250 ml brown stock	

1 Oven 350°F/Gas Mark 4.
2 Wipe meat. Cut into thin slices, remove excess fat.
3 Place in a casserole dish. Slice onions into rings, place on the meat. Add seasoning and stock.
4 Cover, cook 1–1½ hrs. till tender.
5 Drain off the liquid. Thicken as for brown stew.
6 Serve meat and onion on an oval plate garnished with parsley and grilled tomatoes. Serve the sauce in a sauce boat.

CHUCK STEAK CASSEROLE

500 g chuck steak	*2 tomatoes*
25 g seasoned flour	*250 ml brown stock*
120 g mushrooms	*Seasoning*
1 onion	*Bay leaf*

1 Oven 350°F/Gas Mark 4.
2 Wipe the meat, trim off excess fat. Cut into thin slices or cubes.
3 Put the meat and flour into a casserole dish. Cover, and shake until the meat is completely coated with flour.
4 Slice the onion and mushrooms, blanch and slice the tomatoes. Place all the vegetables on the meat.
5 Add stock, seasoning and bay leaf.
6 Cover. Cook 1½–2 hrs. till tender. Serve in the dish in which it was cooked, clean the dish before serving.

HOT POT

500 g neck of beef or mutton	*725 g potatoes*
1–2 medium onions	*Seasoning*
2 carrots	*Stock or water*

1 Oven 350°F/Gas Mark 4.
2 Wipe meat, cut into cubes, remove gristle and excess fat.
3 Prepare vegetables, slice thinly.
4 Put alternate layers of vegetables and meat in a casserole dish; season each layer. The top layer should be potatoes, neatly arranged so as to overlap.
5 Add stock or water to reach ⅔ of the way up the contents of the casserole.
6 Cover, cook 1½–2 hrs. for mutton, 2½–3 hrs. for beef.
7 About ¾ hr. before cooking is completed, remove the casserole lid and allow the potatoes to brown.

8 Serve in the same dish, clean the edge before serving. Serve a green vegetable to complete the course.

BEEF OLIVES

> 500 g lean beef e.g. topside
> or braising steak
> Seasoning
> 1 small onion
>
> Stuffing:
> 15 g margarine for sweating
> ½ small onion diced
> 50 g breadcrumbs
> 1 teasp. chopped parsley
>
> 50 g dripping or lard
> 500 ml brown stock
> Bouquet garni
> 25 g flour
>
> Pinch of thyme
> 15 g suet
> Seasoning
> ½ egg to bind

1 Melt margarine, sweat diced onion till tender. Prepare stuffing, mixing all ingredients to a fairly stiff consistency.
2 Wipe the meat. Cut into thin slices across the grain.
3 Trim to 8 cm x 10 cm. Add any trimmings to the stuffing. Season the slices of meat. Spread the stuffing on the meat. Roll up and tie with string.
4 Slice onion, melt the dripping. Fry the meat to a light brown colour.
5 Add the onion, fry till golden brown.
6 Add the stock, seasoning, bouquet garni. Bring to the boil. Cover. Simmer 1½–2 hrs. (This dish may be cooked in the oven in a casserole dish.)
7 Remove bouquet garni and meat, take off string.
8 Thicken as for brown stew. Serve the meat on an oval plate. Gravy may be poured around or served separately.

FRICASSEE OF CHICKEN OR RABBIT

> 1 chicken or rabbit
> Seasoning
> Bouquet garni
> ½ teasp. lemon juice
> 250 ml water, chicken stock
> or milk
>
> 1 onion
> 25 g plain flour
> 25 g margarine
> 1 tablesp. chopped parsley for
> garnish

1 Cut the chicken or rabbit into small joints. Place in a pan.
2 Cover with water, chicken stock or milk, add seasoning, bouquet garni, lemon juice and chopped onion.
3 Simmer till tender—chicken 45 mins.–1 hr., rabbit 1½–2 hrs.

4 Strain off the stock. Make a roux sauce with the flour, margarine and stock or milk (see sauces).
5 Replace the meat, season and re-heat.
6 Arrange on an oval dish, garnish with parsley.

BRAISED TOPSIDE OF BEEF

500 g lean topside, thick flank
or brisket
Mirepoix:
25 g lard or dripping
100 g carrots
¼ small swede

1 onion
Bouquet garni
Seasoning
500 ml brown stock
25 g cornflour

1 Oven 350°F/Gas Mark 4.
2 Wipe the meat. Trim and tie the joint.
3 Melt the fat and quickly brown the meat on all sides.
4 Remove meat. Dice the vegetables. Place in the pan, fry to absorb the fat. Replace the meat. Add the bouquet garni, seasoning, stock, the liquid to just cover the mirepoix. Cover.
5 Place in the oven 2–2½ hrs. till tender. Baste frequently. Remove the joint and bouquet garni. Drain off the liquid, thicken as for brown stew, using the cornflour.
6 Remove the string from the joint. Serve on an oval plate with the gravy in a boat. Vegetables are discarded.

CURRY

500 g stewing meat (chuck steak, shin beef or minced beef or neck of mutton)
25 g lard or dripping
250 g onions
25 g curry powder (amount to vary with individual taste)
25 g flour or cornflour

15 g tomato purée (optional)
500 ml brown stock or water
25 g chutney (mango if possible)
1 tablesp. desiccated coconut
1 tablesp. sultanas
1 small apple, chopped

1 Wipe the meat, trim fat. Cut into even sized pieces.
2 Melt the fat in a saucepan. Fry the meat till brown. Chop the onions, add, cover and sweat for 10 mins. Drain off any surplus fat.
3 Add the curry powder and flour, blend well and cook for 2 mins.
4 Add the tomato purée and gradually the stock.

5 Bring to the boil, add the rest of the ingredients. Cover.
   Simmer on the top of the stove or in a casserole dish in
   the oven (350°F/Gas Mark 4) 1½–2 hrs. till tender.
6 Taste before serving, add more curry powder and cook a
   further 10 mins. if necessary. Correct the consistency, add
   more liquid or thickening if needed.
   Serve on an oval dish with boiled patna rice round the
   outside (see below).
   Accompaniments for curry—small dishes holding the following:
   chutney, sliced banana in lemon juice, quarters of orange,
   coconut, sultanas, lemon wedges, tomato slices, yoghurt.

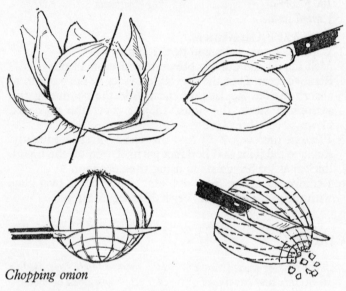

Chopping onion

PATNA RICE

150 g patna rice   Salt
At least 1½ litres water

1 Wash the rice in a sieve.
2 Boil the salted water, add the rice, boil 10–12 mins., till
   tender when bitten. Do not overcook or the grains will
   stick together.
3 Strain. Pour boiling water or cold water through the rice
   to separate the grains.
4 Drain. Keep hot by covering and placing sieve holding the
   rice over a pan of boiling water, fork through occasionally.

MEAT LOAF

Raspings to coat   *1 egg*
1 small onion   *½ teasp. mixed herbs*
500 g minced beef   *Seasoning*
100 g breadcrumbs   *1 teasp. Worcester Sauce*
125 ml stock or water

1 Oven 350°F/Gas Mark 4.
2 Grease a loaf tin 15 cm long and dust with raspings.
3 Grate the onion, mix all the ingredients to give a dropping consistency.
4 Press this mixture well into the tin, leaving no air spaces.
5 Cover with foil or greaseproof paper and bake ¾ hr–1 hr. until firm to the touch.
   Serve with tomato sauce.

HAMBURGERS

1 small onion   *Seasoning*
250 g minced beef   *½ egg*

1 Grate onion, wash mince.
2 Mix the minced meat with the other ingredients, beating it smooth and pressing well together.
3 Divide the mixture into small cakes no more than .5 cm thick (about 8). Press well together.
4 Fry in shallow fat about 10 mins. until firm. Turn once during cooking.
5 The hamburgers may be served in hot rolls or with a barbecue or tomato sauce as a main meal dish.

SPAGHETTI À LA BOLOGNESE

1 small onion   *125 ml stock*
1 small stick celery   *1 teasp. Worcester sauce*
50 g mushrooms   *Seasoning*
25 g vegetable fat or oil   *250 g minced beef*
25 g flour   *250 g spaghetti*
125 ml pulped tomato, fresh or   *15 g margarine*
tinned
        Serve grated Parmesan cheese as an accompaniment.

1 Dice onion, celery and mushrooms.
2 Heat the fat or oil in a saucepan; gently fry the vegetables 5 mins. then stir in the flour.

3 Add the tomatoes, stock, sauce, seasoning and minced beef. Cover, simmer ¾ hr. Taste and re-season if required.
4 Boil the spaghetti in salted water 20 mins. till soft. Drain, add the margarine and shake.
5 Place the spaghetti round the edge of an oval plate. Pour the meat sauce in the middle. Hand the cheese separately.

SHEPHERD'S PIE

500 g minced beef
1 large onion
Seasoning
250 ml stock
500–750 g potatoes

Knob of margarine
2–4 tablesp. milk
Parsley and/or slice of tomato
for garnish

1 Dice onion, place in a saucepan with the meat, seasoning and stock.
2 Bring to the boil. Simmer ¾ hr. till tender.
3 Scrub and peel the potatoes. Boil 20 mins. till soft. Drain, mash with seasoning, margarine and milk.
4 Drain the stock from the meat and place meat in a pie dish, adding two tablesp. stock. Cover the top with potato, either smoothing over and then forking or by using a savoy tube. Grill till golden, garnish with parsley or sliced tomato. Use the stock for gravy.
Skinned sliced tomatoes or mushrooms may be cooked with the meat mixture. Grated cheese may be sprinkled on the potato before grilling.

N.B. Shepherd's Pie may be a réchauffé, i.e. made using left-over cooked meat and potato.

GOULASH

500 g stewing beef
2 onions
2 large tomatoes or 125 ml
tinned tomato
25 g lard
2–4 teasp. paprika pepper
1 teasp. caraway seeds (optional)
    Parsley for garnish

500 ml water
Salt
375 g potatoes
3 tablesp. yoghurt or
3 tablesp. milk soured with
1 teasp. vinegar
25 g flour
1 green pepper (optional)

1 Cut the meat into 2 cm cubes, slice onion thinly, skin and slice fresh tomatoes.
2 Heat the fat and fry the meat quickly till just brown, remove it, fry the onions gently till soft, stir in the paprika pepper and caraway seeds if used.
3 Add the tomatoes, water, salt, replace the meat and simmer the stew 1½–2 hrs. until tender.
4 Three-quarters of an hour before serving, add the peeled and quartered potatoes.
5 Blend the yoghurt with the flour, stir into the stew, cook 5 mins.
6 Taste and season the goulash and serve it in a casserole sprinkled with chopped parsley.
7 The green pepper if used must be de-seeded, shredded and added before thickening.

STEAK AND KIDNEY PIE (kidney may be omitted)

500 g stewing beef
100 g kidney
120 g onions
125 ml litre stock or water
Seasoning

100 g short crust or rough puff or flaky pastry (see pastries)
Beaten egg for glazing

1 Wipe and cut the meat into 2 cm cubes. Slice onions.
2 Place the meat and onions in a covered pan with stock or water and seasoning and simmer 1½ hrs. till tender. More stock may be added if necessary.
3 Prepare the pastry.
4 Oven 425°F/Gas Mark 7.
5 Place meat in a pie dish. The meat should be heaped in the middle to support the pastry. Add enough of the liquid from the meat to come half-way up the pie dish.
6 Roll out the pastry a little larger than the pie dish. Trim to size and use the trimmings to line the dampened edge of the dish. Damp the trimmings.
7 Place the pastry on the dish. Seal and finish the edges. Cut a slit in the centre. Decorate with leaves made from scraps of pastry.
8 Brush with beaten egg.
9 Cook 25–30 mins. till the pastry is golden brown.

N.B. 50–100 g mushrooms may be sliced and cooked with the meat.

STEAK AND KIDNEY PUDDING

250 g suet pastry (see pastries) *seasoning*
500 g stewing beef   *1 dstsp. flour*
50–100 g kidney   *125 ml water (approx.)*
1 small onion

1 Prepare a steamer.
2 Grease a 1 litre pudding basin.
3 Make the pastry, use $\frac{3}{4}$ of it to line the basin.
4 Mix all the other ingredients together and place in the basin, with the water to come within 2 cm of the top.
5 Moisten the edge of the pastry, roll the remaining $\frac{1}{4}$ to form a lid.
   Place on the meat; seal well.
6 Cover with foil or greased greaseproof paper.
7 Cook 3–3$\frac{1}{2}$ hrs. in a steamer. Turn out on to an oval plate.
8 Serve with gravy.

N.B. The meat for this may be pre-cooked for one hour beforehand and the cooking time may be reduced.

MEAT AND POTATO PIE

375 g stewing beef   *250 g potatoes*
250 ml stock   *100 g short crust or flaky*
Seasoning   *pastry*
1 large onion   *Beaten egg for glazing*
2 carrots (optional)

1 Oven 425°F/Gas Mark 7.
2 Prepare the meat, wipe, remove fat and gristle, cut into even-sized pieces (2 cm cubes). Place in a saucepan, cover with stock, add seasoning. Simmer 1$\frac{1}{2}$–2 hrs. till tender.
3 Prepare vegetables, slice onions and carrots and cut potatoes into even-sized pieces.
4 Cook in salted water till tender, drain, place in a pie dish.
5 Drain the meat, add to the pie dish with six tablesp. of stock, season. Use the stock to make the gravy by thickening with cornflour.
6 Prepare the pastry. Roll out a little larger than the pie dish. Trim, use the trimmings to line the dampened edge of the dish. Damp the trimmings. Place the pastry on top of the pie dish. Seal, finish the edges. Cut a hole in the top. Decorate with pastry leaves. Brush with beaten egg.

7 Cook 25 mins. till golden brown.
8 Serve with a green vegetable and gravy.

CORNISH PASTIES

125 g minced beef   *1 small potato*
1 small onion   *250 g short crust pastry*
125 ml water   *Beaten egg for glazing*
Seasoning

1 Oven 425°F/Gas Mark 7.
2 Wash the meat. Chop the onion. Place in a saucepan, add the water and seasoning. Simmer half an hour till tender. Drain.
3 Grate the potato, add the meat and onion mixture to it and season.
4 Prepare the pastry, roll out thinly, cut into large rounds, 10 cm (about 8–10).
5 Place the filling in the middle of each round. Damp the edges of the pastry. Fold over, seal and flute. The pasties may lie flat or stand up with the join on top. Brush with beaten egg.
6 Place on a baking sheet. Cook 20–25 mins. till golden brown.
7 Serve hot with vegetables and gravy or cold with salad for high tea, picnics or packed lunches.

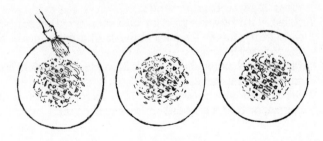

Cornish pasties—final shaping

SAUSAGE ROLLS

250 g short crust pastry or   250 g sausage meat
flaky pastry   Beaten egg for glazing

1 Oven 425°F/Gas Mark 7.
2 Make the pastry. Roll out into a rectangle approximately
   24 cm x 12 cm.
3 Trim off the edges and cut the pastry into half, lengthwise.
4 Divide the sausage meat into two and roll each piece on a
   floured board to the same length as the pastry.
5 Put a roll of sausage meat on each piece of pastry.
6 Damp one edge of each piece of pastry. Fold over the
   other edge, seal and decorate.
7 Brush with beaten egg. Cut into even-sized pieces (small
   for a party, larger for packed meals or a main meal). Snip
   the tops with scissors.
8 Place on a baking sheet. Cook 25 mins. till golden brown
   and firm underneath.
9 Serve hot on an oval dish with vegetables as a main
   course, or cold with salad or for a packed meal.

(See illustration opposite.)

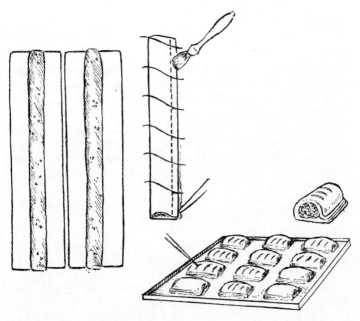

Preparation of sausage rolls

BAKED GAMMON

1 joint of gammon
½ teasp. mustard
Bay leaf
Demerara sugar or raspings

Cloves
Pineapple rings or peach halves or apricot halves

1 Soak the joint overnight in cold water to remove excess salt.
2 Wash the meat, place in a large saucepan and add bay leaf and mustard, then water to cover. Boil 25 mins. per 500 g. Remove from the water and strip off the skin.
3 Score the fat into squares. Press on the brown sugar or raspings and stud with cloves.
4 Bake in the oven, 400°F/Gas Mark 6, in a roasting tin 30 mins. or until tender.
5 The fruit may be placed round the meat or grilled separately.
6 Serve on an oval plate with the fruit around. A white sauce or a sauce made by thickening the fruit juice with arrowroot or cornflour may be served. (250 ml juice to 15 g cornflour or arrowroot (see sauces)).

Offal

Liver

Ox Liver: usually the cheapest, it may have a very strong flavour and is always coarse in texture. Not suitable for grilling and frying, but it can be stewed or casseroled.

Calves' liver: usually the most expensive and the finest in texture. Delicate in flavour. It is best fried or grilled. Over-cooking makes it tough, hard and dry.

Lambs' liver: cheaper than calves' and has a stronger flavour. Suitable for frying, grilling, casseroling. Over-cooking makes it tough.

Pigs' liver: a little cheaper than lambs' liver and has a stronger flavour. Good for casseroles, etc.

Kidney

Ox: fairly tough and strong, usually stewed or used in soups, pies, etc.

Lambs' or pigs': tender, usually skinned, split in half, core removed and then grilled or fried.

Tripe—requires long, slow cooking. Recipe on p. 58.

SAVOURY LIVER

300 g pigs, lamb or ox liver	125 g breadcrumbs
1 or 2 onions	4–6 rashers bacon
Seasoning	½ teasp. mixed herbs
Water	1 tablesp. chopped parsley
½ tablesp. seasoned flour	Nutmeg

1 Oven 350°F/Gas Mark 4.
2 Wash, dry and slice the liver thinly. Remove any skin and blood vessels.
3 Peel onion, cut into two and boil 10 mins. in salted water.
4 Dip the liver in the seasoned flour and place the slices in a casserole dish. Remove bacon rind.
5 Chop the onion finely, mix with the crumbs, herbs and seasoning.
6 Sprinkle liver with the crumb mixture and arrange the bacon on top.
7 Pour in enough water to come half-way up the crumbs.
8 Cook ¾ hr. for lambs' or pigs' liver, 1 hr. for ox until tender.

9 Serve in the same dish. Add a vegetable to the meal containing a large amount of vitamin C, as this helps the absorption of iron.

LIVER RISOTTO (2 servings)

1 onion	100 g patna rice
25 g margarine	Approx. 500 ml stock
2 tomatoes	½ teasp. mixed herbs
2 rashers streaky bacon	Seasoning
125 g liver	

1 Chop the onion finely, melt the margarine in a frying pan and sweat the onion 5 mins. Blanch the tomatoes.
2 Remove rind and chop the bacon. Fry till clear. Wash skin, chop the liver and fry gently for 3 mins.
3 Add the rice, cook 2 mins.
4 Chop the tomatoes and add, together with 125 ml stock, herbs and seasoning.
5 Simmer gently without a lid, stirring and adding more stock gradually to keep it moist.
6 Continue cooking until the rice is tender and the risotto is still moist, about 20–30 mins.
7 Taste, re-season if required. Serve hot on a deep dish.

N.B. Chopped cooked ham or cooked chicken may be used instead of liver.

FRIED LIVER AND ONIONS

300 g liver (calf, pig or lamb)	2 onions
Seasoned flour	4 rashers bacon (optional)
15 g lard	250 ml stock

1 Wash, dry, slice the liver thinly. Remove skin and blood vessels. Coat in seasoned flour.
2 Melt the lard in a frying pan. Fry the liver gently 5–7 mins. till tender, turning once, drain.
3 Slice the onions thinly and fry till tender, drain.
4 The bacon, if used, may be fried or grilled.
5 Use the sediment in the pan and 1 tablesp. flour plus stock to make the gravy.
6 Serve on an oval plate, onions over or around the liver. Gravy in a sauceboat. Add a vegetable rich in Vitamin C.

TRIPE AND ONIONS

250 g tripe
2 onions
Seasoning
25 g margarine

25 g plain flour
250 ml milk and water
Parsley for garnish

1 Wash the tripe. Cut into small pieces.
2 Slice the onion.
3 Put in a saucepan and cover with milk or water. Add seasoning.
4 Simmer 1½–2 hrs. till tender.
5 Strain. Use the stock to make a white roux sauce (see sauces), using margarine, flour and the stock (250 mls). Strain.
6 Add the tripe and onions to the sauce, re-season if necessary, serve in a casserole dish. Garnish with parsley.

FRIED CHICKEN

Chicken portion 1 or 2 per person
Seasoned flour
Beaten egg and bread-crumbs for coating

Fried bananas
bacon rolls
sweet corn
chipped potatoes
watercress as accompaniments

1 Coat joints in seasoned flour, then in beaten egg and breadcrumbs.
2 Fry in shallow or deep fat, 15–20 mins. till golden and tender. Drain well on absorbent paper.
3 Serve on a hot oval dish with accompaniments.

GRILLED CHICKEN

Chicken portions 1 or 2 per person

Melted fat for brushing

1 Brush the joints with melted fat.
2 Pre-heat a grill to a medium heat. Grill 10 mins. each side till golden brown and tender. Drain well on absorbent paper.
3 Serve in a basket or on a hot oval dish.

CASSEROLED CHICKEN

4 chicken portions or 1   *100 g mushrooms*
jointed chicken   *1 tablesp. tomato purée*
100 g seasoned flour   *500 ml stock*
25 g lard or dripping   *Seasoning*
1 onion   *Bouquet garni*

1 Coat chicken in seasoned flour, reserving the remainder. Melt the fat in a shallow pan and fry the chicken until golden-brown. Remove from pan.
2 Dice the onion—slice the mushrooms and fry until tender.
3 Add flour, stirring, and cook till golden brown.
4 Add the tomato purée and stock gradually. Bring to the boil. Season.
5 Place the chicken in a casserole, pour sauce over, add the bouquet garni. Cover. Cook 1½–2 hrs. till the chicken is tender. Remove bouquet garni.

CHICKEN PASTIES

100 g minced cooked chicken   *1 large potato*
1 chicken stock cube for   *½ onion*
seasoning

Proceed as for Cornish Pasties (p. 53) omitting the cooking of the meat.

BARBECUED CHICKEN

1½ kilo chicken   *1 sprig parsley*
Seasoning   *Melted fat for brushing*
Bay leaf   *500 ml barbecue sauce (see p.*
1 chopped onion   *207)*

1 Prepare a rotisserie to a medium heat.
2 Wash the chicken. Season, inside and out.
3 Place the bay leaf, chopped onion and sprig of parsley inside the bird. Place the chicken on the bar of the rotisserie.
4 Brush the outside of the chicken with melted fat. Allow to rotate 1½ hrs. till tender and golden brown. Baste in fat every 20 mins.

5 Remove bay leaf, parsley and onion.
6 Serve whole or in joints with the barbecue sauce.
N.B. If no rotisserie is available, the chicken may be oven roasted in the normal way or jointed and grilled. (See grilled chicken p. 58).

CHICKEN PIE

200 g short crust pastry	*50 g mushrooms*
1 green pepper	*500 g cooked chicken*
1 large onion	*125 ml chicken stock*

1 Oven 425°F/Gas Mark 7.
2 Roll out the pastry to cover a 1 litre pie dish.
3 Remove top and seeds from pepper. Dice. Chop onion and mushroom. Cut chicken into equal size pieces.
4 Place chicken, vegetables, seasoning and stock into the pie dish. Cover with pastry as for fruit pie (see p. 98).
5 Bake for 20 mins. Turn oven down to 375°F/Gas Mark 5 for a further 10–15 mins. till the pastry is golden brown and crisp and the vegetables are tender.

BRAISED CHICKEN

A mirepoix consisting of 1 carrot, piece of swede, 1 stick celery, 1 onion (50 g mushrooms and 1 green pepper may be added if liked).

25 g margarine	*Seasoning*
500 ml water	*1 chicken stock cube*
1 boiling chicken	*Bouquet garni*

1 Dice carrot, swede, onion and celery (chop mushrooms and chop green pepper if used).
2 Melt the margarine in a saucepan.
3 Sauté the vegetables until golden brown. Add the liquid. Bring to boiling point. Weigh the chicken.
4 Place the chicken in the liquid, add seasoning, stock cube and bouquet garni. Baste the chicken with the liquid. Cover with a tight fitting lid.
5 Simmer on top of the stove or in a moderate oven

350°F/Gas Mark 4, allowing 1 hour to each kilo, basting the chicken every 20 mins.
6 Drain the liquid. Serve the chicken on an oval plate with freshly cooked vegetables. The liquid may be used as a sauce and the vegetables discarded or the whole thickened and served as a soup.

CHICKEN MARYLAND

1 chicken about 1½ kilos or 4   ½ *teasp. salt*
chicken quarters   ¼ *teasp. paprika*
100 g seasoned flour   *2 tablesp. top of milk*
Egg and breadcrumbs for   *Corn fritters*
coating   *fried bananas (see later),*
125 g lard, dripping or oil   *potato croquettes (see potato)*
500 ml chicken stock   *Watercress to serve*

1 Joint whole chicken—coat each chicken portion with seasoned flour. Save the remaining flour.
2 Coat—egg and breadcrumbs.
3 Heat lard, dripping or oil in a shallow pan till it is hot enough to brown a piece of bread in 2 mins.
4 Fry the portions of chicken till golden brown and tender. Drain and keep hot on an oval dish.
5 Pour off most of the fat, leaving sufficient to coat the bottom of a pan. Heat gently and stir in the remaining seasoned flour, cooking to a sandy brown colour.
6 Add the stock, stirring. Boil. Add salt and paprika and taste.
7 Return to the heat, adding the top of milk. Heat, do not boil.
8 Pour over the chicken and serve garnished with corn fritters, fried bananas, potato croquettes and watercress.

FRIED BANANAS

1 Cut bananas into half lengthways, then into pieces.
2 Drop into hot fat. Fry until pale golden, drain.

CORN FRITTERS

100 g S.R. flour   *1 egg beaten with 3 tablesp.*
¼ *teasp. salt*   *milk*
15 g margarine   *1 small can sweetcorn*

1 Mix flour and salt, add margarine, rub in.
2 Add the egg and milk.
3 Drain the sweetcorn and add. Mix well to make a smooth batter.
4 Melt some lard or oil in a frying pan. Heat until it will brown bread in 2 mins.
5 Drop in tablesp. of batter. Cook on one side till golden, then turn over and brown on the second side.
6 Drain. Serve on a hot oval dish.

9

Cheese, eggs and savouries

QUICHE LORRAINE

100 g short crust pastry   *125 ml milk*
2 rashers bacon   *Seasoning*
1 onion   *25 g cheese*
15 g lard   *Parsley for garnish*
1 egg

1 Oven 400°F/Gas Mark 6. Place a 14 cm flan ring on a baking sheet.
2 Make the pastry, line the flan ring, being careful not to pierce the pastry.
3 Rind, fry and chop the bacon. Dice the onion, melt the lard and fry till tender. Drain.
4 Place the bacon and onion in the flan case. Beat the egg and milk, add seasoning and pour into the pastry. Grate the cheese and sprinkle on top.
5 Cook 25–30 mins. till set and the pastry is golden. If necessary remove the flan ring to brown the pastry.
6 Serve hot with vegetables and garnished with parsley, or cool and serve with a salad or slice for packed meals.

SAVOURY FLAN

100 g short crust pastry   *Seasoning*
125 ml milk plus filling   *1 egg*
Fillings any of the following:
  50 g mushrooms sliced and fried
  25 g grated cheese and 1 onion diced
  75 g grated cheese and 1–2

tomatoes skinned and sliced
1 small tin shrimps

Make as for Quiche Lorraine.

CHEESE FLAN

100 g cheese pastry	*1–2 cooked carrots*
2 tablesp. cooked peas	*1–2 hard boiled eggs*
2 skinned tomatoes	*250 ml coating cheese*
15 g grated cheese	*Sauce (white roux)*
	Parsley for garnish

1 Oven 400°F/Gas Mark 6. Place a 14 cm flan ring on a baking sheet.
2 Make the pastry, line the flan ring.
3 Prick, cover with greased greaseproof paper and baking beans. Bake blind 20 mins. Just before the pastry is firm and golden, remove the paper and beans.
4 Make the sauce.
5 Slice the carrots, tomatoes, egg and arrange in layers with the peas in the flan case. Between each layer of vegetables, add cheese sauce, finishing with sauce.
6 Sprinkle with grated cheese on top of the sauce.
7 Brown in the oven 15 mins. or under the grill if the ingredients are hot. Garnish with parsley, serve hot or cold with vegetables, or salad.

CHEESE PUDDING (2 portions)

50 g breadcrumbs	*1 egg*
250 ml milk	*50 g grated cheese*
Seasonings	*1 tomato for garnish*
¼ teasp. mustard	*Parsley for garnish*

1 Oven 375°F/Gas Mark 5. Grease a 500 ml pie dish.
2 Beat the egg or separate the yolk and white and beat the yolk.
3 Warm the milk and add with cheese and seasonings to the egg. Pour over the breadcrumbs, cool.
4 If the white was separated, whisk it to a peak and fold into the breadcrumbs.
5 Pour into the dish, cook 30 mins. till just set and golden. Slice tomato and use for garnish with parsley.

MACARONI OR SPAGHETTI CHEESE
(2 servings)

50 g macaroni or spaghetti   *1 tomato*
Seasoning   *1 round of toast or fried bread*
250 ml white coating sauce   *Parsley for garnish*
50 g grated cheese

1 Break macaroni or spaghetti into pieces and cook in boiling salted water about 20 mins. till tender. Strain.
2 Make the sauce by the roux method (see sauces), add half the cheese and the macaroni or spaghetti, season well, place in a pie or casserole dish.
3 Sprinkle the rest of the cheese on the surface. Arrange sliced tomato on top. Grill or brown in the oven.
4 Cut the toast into triangles. Arrange round the edge of the dish. Serve hot, garnished with parsley.

EGGS AU GRATIN

4 eggs   *1 tablesp. breadcrumbs*
250 ml white coating sauce   *Parsley and tomato for*
100 g grated cheese   *garnish*

1 Hard boil eggs, 10 mins. Cool. Shell, cut into half lengthways, place in an oven-proof dish.
2 Make a coating roux sauce. Add half the grated cheese. Pour over the eggs. Sprinkle the rest of the cheese with the breadcrumbs on top.
3 Grill till golden brown. Garnish with parsley and sliced tomato. Serve hot.

CAULIFLOWER AU GRATIN

1 cauliflower   *100 g grated cheese*
250 ml white coating sauce   *Parsley for garnish*
1 tablesp. breadcrumbs

1 Prepare and boil cauliflower whole, 20 mins., till tender. (see vegetables).
2 Finish as for eggs au gratin. Garnish with parsley, use as a high tea or supper dish.

BAKED EGGS

4 eggs   *50 g butter (not margarine)*
Salt

1 Oven 325°F/Gas Mark 3.
2 Divide the butter into four pieces. Place in a dish or in four individual dishes.
3 Break each egg into a cup, add a pinch of salt.
4 Slide each egg on top of a piece of butter.
5 Bake 10 mins. or until whites are set.
6 Serve with toast.

SCOTCH EGGS

To each egg, 50 g sausage   *Beaten egg*
meat   *Raspings*
Flour

1 Hard boil eggs, 10 mins. Cool. Shell and dust with flour.
2 Shape each piece of sausage meat into a flat round cake. Wrap round egg, keeping an even thickness and pressing out all cracks.
3 Coat with egg and raspings twice.
4 Heat lard or oil in a deep pan until it will brown bread in 50 secs.
5 Fry eggs 7–10 mins. till golden and the sausage meat is cooked. Drain on absorbent paper.
6 Cut in half lengthways. Serve hot with vegetables or cool, cut in half lengthways and serve with salad.

SAUSAGE, EGG AND TOMATO PIE

200 g short crust pastry   *200 g sausage meat*
2 tomatoes   *Beaten egg for glazing*
1–2 hard-boiled eggs

1 Oven 400°F/Gas Mark 6.
2 Make the pastry and use two-thirds to line a 15 cm sandwich tin.
3 Blanch the tomatoes, slice. Shell and slice the eggs.
4 Spread the sausage meat on the pastry, cover with eggs and tomatoes.
5 Damp the pastry edges. Use the remaining third to make a lid. Press and flute the edge.
6 Brush with beaten egg. Bake 40–45 mins. till golden. Serve hot or cold with vegetables or salad.

EGG CURRY

4 hard-boiled eggs	*15 g desiccated coconut*
1 onion	*150 g patna rice*
15 g margarine	*½ apple*
15 g or more curry powder	*250 ml stock*
15 g flour	*15 g sultanas*
1 teasp. mango chutney	
(other curry accompaniments see *meat)*	

1 Shell, cool and halve eggs. Place in a dish.
2 Chop onion finely and apple coarsely.
3 Melt the margarine and fry onion gently, do not brown.
4 Add curry powder and flour and cook 2–3 mins.
5 Add the apple, chutney, coconut, sultanas and stock. Stir till the sauce simmers.
6 Cook 15 mins. till the apple is tender.
7 Pour over the eggs. Serve hot with accompaniments and patna rice.

BOILED EGGS

1 Heat enough water to cover the eggs in a small pan.
2 Boil gently, lower the eggs into the pan carefully.
3 Bring back to the boil. Time to suit individual tastes, 3–6 mins. Lift out. Serve in an egg cup, with toast or bread and butter. To hard boil—boil 10 mins. and cool under running water. Shell.

POACHED EGGS

Can be cooked in an egg poaching pan or as follows:
1 Make some toast, butter, keep hot.
2 Half fill a frying pan with water and bring just to the boil.
3 Break each egg into a cup.
4 Slide egg into the water or grease a plain metal cutter, stand it in the water, and pour the egg into that.
5 Baste the top of the egg with water and simmer 2–3 mins. till the white is set. Remove with a fish slice.
6 Serve on the toast.

SCRAMBLED EGGS

To each person allow 1–2   *1 round of bread for toasting*
eggs   *Butter to spread*
15 g margarine or butter   *Seasoning*
1 tablesp. milk

1 Make the toast, butter, keep hot.
2 Beat the eggs lightly, add seasoning and milk.
3 Melt the margarine in a saucepan.
4 Add the egg and stir with a wooden spoon over gentle heat.
5 Remove from the heat when the egg begins to set. Cooking is finished by the heat of the pan. While the mixture is still creamy, pile it on the toast. Garnish with parsley.

N.B. It is very easy to overcook scrambled eggs. Remove them from the heat before they are ready and do not leave in the pan or the egg protein will over-coagulate and become rubbery.

To vary the dish, just before serving add one of the following: 1 small tomato peeled and sliced; or 1 teasp. chopped parsley, or chopped ham or grated cheese.

FRIED EGGS

1 Melt some lard in a frying pan, wait until it melts.
2 Crack in the eggs, tipping the pan to prevent the white spreading.
3 Baste the top of the egg with the hot fat, using a spoon. Cook until the white is set and the yolk takes on a faint pink colour.
4 Remove with a fish slice. Drain.
5 Serve on a hot plate with bacon, etc.

WELSH RAREBIT

Slice of bread   *2 tablesp. milk*
15 g butter   *Few drops Worcester sauce*
50 g grated cheese   *Pinch of dry mustard*
Parsley, sliced tomato or fried bacon for garnish

1 Toast the bread on one side only.
2 Melt the butter in a saucepan, add the cheese, milk, Worcester sauce, mustard and seasoning.

3 Heat slowly, stirring, till the cheese has melted.
4 Pour on to the uncooked side of the toast. Grill until golden brown and bubbling.
Garnish with parsley and sliced tomato or a piece of fried bacon.

TO WHISK AN EGG WHITE

To separate the egg, either use a separator or crack the shell with a knife and pull it apart with the thumbs, allowing the white to run out into a clean dry basin. Tip the yolk back and forth into the two halves of the shell to help this. Place the yolk in a second basin.

1 When whisking whites, the cells containing the albumen are broken down and air is entangled. The larger the amount of air trapped and the colder it is, the more expansion occurs on heating and the lighter is the resulting mixture.
2 Grease (including egg yolk) or water in the basin will prevent the white becoming stiff.
3 Whisk in a cool place until the white stands in firm peaks. Whisk in gradually half to all of any caster sugar used and fold in the rest if any. Always use caster sugar, not granulated, as caster dissolves more easily.
4 Fold lightly into the mixture. Cook immediately so as to prevent the air escaping.

OMELETS

Fillings any one of the following:
25 g grated cheese
50–100 g chopped and fried mushrooms
1 sliced onion, cooked
1 sliced skinned tomato
50 g chopped cooked ham
Mixed herbs, fresh if possible (very small quantity)
3 eggs   Seasoning
*   15 g butter (not margarine)*

1 Prepare filling, keep hot if cooked.
2 Prove an omelet pan: sprinkle salt in the pan, heat gently. Clean with paper and a cloth. Melt a piece of lard the size

of a walnut in the pan. Heat until the fat darkens. Allow the fat to run over the pan. Pour away the fat.

3 Beat the eggs well and season.

4 Melt the butter until it sizzles. Pour the egg slowly into the fat. Stir with the back of a fork, keeping it pressed against the pan, shaking the pan in the meantime over a moderate heat.

5 As the omelet begins to set, stop stirring, and when the under-side is golden and the surface is creamy, add the filling, fold over the nearside to the centre and slide on to a hot plate. Serve immediately.

N.B. The most important point is not to overcook, as the egg protein over-coagulates, becoming tough and rubbery. 2–3 mins. is sufficient.

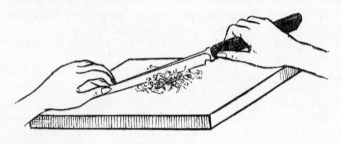

Chopping herbs

SANDWICHES

Making

1 Bread should be one day old.

2 Crusts may be removed before slicing and buttering.

3 Butter should be softened before using. Work with a knife on a plate.

4 250 g butter spreads approximately 22 large slices (1 sliced loaf).

5 Bread can be white, brown, rye, granary or in the form of rolls or cobs, etc.

6 Work to a method; prepare the fillings first, season, soften the butter, slice the bread, spread on the butter, place slices, butter sides together. Use all one filling at a time. Press well, cut. Arrange sandwiches on an oval or sandwich plate. Garnish.

Cutting sandwiches

Squares—cut into 4

Diamonds—cut an equilateral triangle from each corner, thus leaving a diamond shape in the middle.

Bridge sandwiches—cut with small cutters shaped as diamonds, hearts, spades and clubs.

Rolls—cut thin slices of fresh bread, spread and roll up.

Pin-wheels—as for rolls, then slice like a Swiss roll.

Layers—four to six layers of different breads with various coloured fillings. Wrap in damp greaseproof or foil, press well, cut.

Checker board—cut 8 long strips, 4 cm wide, from a white loaf. Cut each strip into cubes 4 cm. Repeat with brown bread. Arrange alternately white and brown as a draught board, making a block of four across and four down. Spread. Repeat with a second 16 pieces and put together.

Open—slightly thicker bread is used. Use slices of egg, ham, salami, cucumber, etc., garnish.

Fillings

Savoury—scrambled egg, hard boiled egg, eggs and cress, eggs and mayonnaise, cheese and celery, cheese and onion, cheese and tomato, cheese and chutney, cottage cheese and cucumber, cottage cheese and date, cheese and raisins, sardines, salmon and cucumber, meat or poultry, salami, sausage, bacon and banana, cooked vegetables in mayonnaise, salad, peanut butter, shrimp, crab, etc.

Sweet—jam, chocolate spread, banana, apple and date, honey, syrup, sweetened condensed milk.

10
Vegetables

The choice and purchase of vegetables
1 Choose in season when vegetables are at their cheapest and best.
2 Use green vegetables within two days of purchase. Vitamin C is lost on storing.
3 Allow for wastage on the weight of vegetables, e.g. Brussels sprouts, spring cabbage, peas, beans, etc.
4 Buy sufficient vegetables for the number of people concerned.
5 Fresh vegetables should be firm and bright in colour, free from bruises and excess soil.

Quantities of vegetables to buy per person, allowing for wastage

Vegetable	Weight/person
Potatoes	250 g
Spring cabbage	250 g
White cabbage	200 g
Brussels sprouts	250 g
Carrots, parsnips, swede, etc.	120 g
Kidney beans	100 g
French beans or peas	250 g
Tomatoes	100 g
Mushrooms	50 g
Cauliflower 1 large	4–6 persons

General rules for the preparation and cooking of vegetables
1 Use all vegetables as fresh as possible.
2 Discard fibrous or withered parts.
3 Soak the green vegetables for no more than 10 mins. in cold salt water to float out slugs. The salt slows up the solution of vitamins and minerals.
4 Rinse thoroughly.

5 Dark outer leaves contain more vitamin A than the inner leaves. Stalks and outer leaves may be cooked for 3 mins. before the main part.

6 Shred or slice vegetables with a large sharp knife, e.g. French cook's knife. A blunt knife will crush and tear cells and cause the release of oxidase.

7 Cook with not quite enough boiling water to cover them.

8 Cook vegetables quickly in the shortest time possible with the lid on the pan.

9 Test vegetables with a sharp pointed skewer to avoid breaking them.

10 Cooking water may be used for sauces or gravies.

11 Avoid use of bicarbonate of soda, as this destroys vitamin C and B.

CONSERVATIVE METHOD OF COOKING VEGETABLES OTHER THAN GREEN VEGETABLES

500 g vegetables e.g. carrots, parsnips, celery, swede, onions
15 g margarine or butter

125 ml boiling water
1 level teasp. salt
Chopped parsley

1 Scrub or peel vegetables. Slice if mature, leave whole if young and tender, e.g. young new carrots.

2 Melt fat in a pan or a casserole dish in the oven.

3 Sweat the vegetables with the lid on the pan for 5–10 mins.

4 Add boiling water. If cooking is carried out in a pan, add all the water. If cooking is carried out in a casserole dish, add half of the water only. Add salt. Place lid on pan. Cover casserole dish with greased paper before placing lid on top.

5 Simmer vegetables gently until tender, 20–30 mins. in the pan, 30–40 mins. in a casserole dish.

6 Serve liquid with the vegetables. Sprinkle with chopped parsley.

CONSERVATIVE METHOD OF COOKING GREEN VEGETABLES

Aim: To preserve soluble nutrients. This is done by cooking quickly in a small quantity of water for the shortest time possible with the lid on the pan.

1 kilo Brussels sprouts, savoy *1 level teasp. salt*
cabbage, spring cabbage, *Nut of margarine or butter*
broccoli or spinach *Water*

1 Prepare the vegetables.
Brussels—remove withered leaves, slit the stalks. Keep whole.
Cabbage—remove withered leaves. Cut savoy cabbage into quarters. Remove stalk. Shred cabbage. Spring cabbage may be shredded whole with the stalk.
Broccoli—Keep the flowering sprays whole. Discard tough stalks. Shred usable stalks. Keep small inner leaves whole.
Spinach—Remove stalks and mid ribs. Keep leaves whole.
2 Soak the prepared vegetables in salt water for 5 mins. to remove any grit or slugs. Dry in a clean tea towel.
3 Place a 1 cm depth of water in a large pan. Add salt. Bring water to the boil.
4 Place the prepared vegetables into the boiling water. Place lid on the pan. Bring water back to a gentle boil.
5 Cook Brussels sprouts   ..   ..   ..   10–12 mins
      Savoy cabbage..   ..   ..   ..   10–15 mins
      spring cabbage..   ..   ..   ..   7–10 mins
      broccoli   ..   ..   10–12 mins
      spinach..   ..   ..   5–10 mins

Cook until leaves are tender but not soggy. Sogginess indicates that the vegetables are overcooked.
6 Strain well in a colander. Stock may be kept for a sauce.
7 Serve at once in a tureen or vegetable dish. Top with butter.

CREAMED POTATOES (4 persons)

1 kilo potatoes *2 tablesp. milk*
500 ml–1 lt water *30 g margarine or butter*
2 teasp. salt *Seasonings*

1 Scrub and peel potatoes. Cut into even sizes.
2 Wash potatoes. Place in a large pan which they $\frac{2}{3}$ fill.
3 Add water, sufficient to cover the potatoes, add salt. Bring water to the boil.
4 Boil potatoes with the lid on the pan for 20–25 mins. Test for tenderness with a skewer. The skewer should penetrate through the potato easily when it is cooked.
5 Drain the water through the lid.

6 Add milk, margarine and seasoning. Cream potatoes with a potato masher until they are free of any lumps. More milk may be added if necessary. Taste. Add any further seasoning if necessary.
7 Place in a tureen or vegetable dish. Smooth over the surface with a palette knife. Decorate with a fork.
8 Garnish with parsley. Serve hot.

NEW POTATOES

1 kilo new potatoes
2 level teasp. salt
Water

Sprig of mint (optional)
1 tablesp. chopped parsley (optional)
25 g margarine or butter

1 Scrape and wash potatoes.
2 Place in a large pan, add salt and sufficient water to cover the potatoes.
3 Bring water to the boil. Add mint if used. Boil for 15 mins. Test with a skewer.
4 Strain, remove mint.
5 Add butter and chopped parsley if used.
6 Replace lid and toss potatoes in butter, and parsley if used.
7 Serve hot in a tureen or vegetable dish.
8 Minted potatoes may be garnished with a sprig of mint.

BOILED CARROTS, PARSNIPS, SWEDES OR TURNIPS

500 g carrots, parsnips, swedes or turnips
1 level teasp. salt
250–500 ml water

1 tablesp. chopped parsley (optional)
Nut of margarine or butter

1 Scrub vegetables. Remove roots and stalks.
2 Scrape if young, or peel with a potato peeler.
3 Slice into fairly thin rings. Rinse in cold water.
4 Place in a medium sized pan. Add salt and water. Bring water to the boil.
5 Boil gently for 20–25 mins. Test with a skewer or fork for tenderness.
6 Strain in a colander. Stock may be used for gravy.

7 Return to the pan. Add chopped parsley if used, and butter. Replace lid. Toss vegetables in butter as for new potatoes.
8 Serve hot in a tureen or vegetable dish.

BOILED BEETROOT

500 g beetroot   Water
1 level teasp. salt

Method 1
1 Do not peel, slice or scrub the beetroot.
2 Cut stalk down to 2 cm length.
3 Place beetroot in a large pan. Add sufficient cold water to cover the beetroot. Add salt.
4 Bring water to the boil. Simmer beetroot for 1–2 hours until tender. Test with a skewer as for potatoes. When beetroot is cooked the skin peels off easily.
5 Strain well in a colander. Remove stalk, rub off the skin.
6 If beetroot is small it may be served whole. If large, slice into thin slices.
7 Serve in a shallow vegetable dish when cold.

Method 2
Ingredients as for Method 1 plus *125 ml vinegar*.
1 Scrape off the skin. Remove stalk. If beetroot are large, slice fairly thinly. Small beetroot may be kept whole.
2 Add 125 ml boiling water. Add salt.
3 Simmer 20–30 mins., until beetroot is soft. Test with a skewer.
4 Drain off 125 ml of the liquid.
5 Place beetroot and remaining liquid in a deep vegetable dish.
6 Add vinegar to the beetroot. Leave to cool in the liquid.
7 Serve with the liquid when cold.

BOILED ONIONS

500 g onions   Either a nut margarine or
250 ml water   butter or 250 ml white coating
1 level teasp. salt   sauce made from half milk
                          half onion water

1 Remove stalk and root. Remove papery skin. Do not soak or wash. Leave small onions whole. Cut large onions into halves or quarters.

2 Place in a medium sized pan with the water and salt.
3 Cover pan. Bring water to the boil. Simmer gently for 20–30 mins. until tender. Test with a skewer.
4 Drain well in a colander. Stock may be kept for sauce.
5 Place in a vegetable dish. Butter may be added or the onions may be served in a coating sauce (see sauces).

BOILED LEEKS

500 g leeks
1 teasp. salt
250 ml water

Nut of butter or 250 ml white coating sauce

1 Remove root and outer layer of leaves. Cut off any withered leaves.
2 Split leeks ¼ down their length, turn back the leaves and wash under running water to remove grit.
3 Tie leeks into a bundle. Place in a large pan. Add salt and water.
4 Place lid on pan. Bring water to the boil. Simmer gently 30–40 mins. until tender. Test with a skewer.
5 Strain, remove string and serve as for boiled onions.

BOILED BEANS (RUNNER OR KIDNEY OR BROAD BEANS) OR PEAS (4 portions)

1 kilo Broad beans or peas or
500 g kidney or runner beans
1 level teasp. salt
250 ml water

1 level teasp. sugar and a sprig of mint may be used when cooking peas
Nut of margarine or butter

1 Shell peas or broad beans. Remove stalk and tip from kidney or runner beans and remove string from the sides. Slice diagonally at ½ cm intervals. Rinse peas or beans in a colander.
2 Place salt and water in a medium sized pan. Add sugar and mint, if used, for peas.
3 Bring water to the boil. Add vegetables.
4 Place lid on pan. Simmer gently. Broad beans 15–30 mins. depending on age. Runner and kidney beans 5–10 mins., peas 10–15 mins.
5 Test by tasting. The vegetables are tender when cooked.
6 Drain well in a colander. Stock may be kept for sauce.

7 Place in a vegetable dish or tureen. Top with butter.
8 Serve at once whilst hot.

BOILED CELERY

1 head celery
125 ml water
1 level teasp. salt

Nut of margarine or butter or
250 ml white coating sauce
made from half milk, half
celery water.

1 Remove green leaves. Cut sticks into 10–12 cm lengths. Rinse in cold water.
2 Place water and salt in a large pan. Bring water to the boil.
3 Place celery in the pan. Cover. Simmer celery 20–30 mins. until celery is tender. Test with a skewer.
4 Strain in a colander. Reserve water for sauce.
5 Place in a vegetable dish. Serve either with a nut of butter or coat with white sauce (see sauces).
6 Serve immediately.

BRAISED CELERY

1 head celery
1 medium sized carrot
½ onion
Small piece swede
½ rasher bacon

25 g dripping
Sufficient water to cover the vegetables
Bouquet garni
1 level teasp. salt

1 Prepare celery as for boiling. Blanch.
2 Prepare other vegetables by peeling and cutting into thick pieces.
3 Cut bacon into 1 cm square pieces.
4 Place the dripping in a medium sized heavy pan. Melt the dripping.
5 Fry bacon in the fat until cooked but not brown.
6 Add the vegetables except celery. Sweat the vegetables gently with the lid on the pan for 10 mins.
7 Add the water to just cover the vegetables. Add bouquet garni and salt.
8 Arrange celery on top of the mirepoix.
9 Replace lid on the pan. Simmer gently for 40–45 mins. until celery is tender. Test with a skewer.
10 Strain well. Reserve vegetable stock for sauce.
11 Serve as for boiled celery with or without a sauce.

ROAST POTATOES

750 g potatoes   *Water*
1 level teasp. salt   *120 g dripping*

1 Oven Gas Mark 7 or 425°F.
2 Scrub and peel potatoes. Cut into even sizes.
3 Place in a large pan with salt and water. Boil for 10 mins.
4 Meanwhile place fat in a roasting tin and place in the oven
   to melt. The fat or dripping must reach hazing point, i.e.
   a blue haze seen to rise from the fat.
5 Strain potatoes in a colander. Shake off any water.
6 Place the potatoes in the fat in the roasting tin. Roll the
   potatoes in the fat so that they are thoroughly basted.
7 Bake for 1 hour, basting every 20 mins. The potatoes are
   cooked when they are golden brown and tender. Test with
   a skewer.
8 Drain on kitchen paper.
9 Serve hot in a vegetable dish or around a roasted joint on
   an oval meat plate.

ROASTED PARSNIPS

500 g parsnips   *Water*
1 level teasp. salt   *100 g lard or dripping*

Follow the method as for roast potatoes but prepare
parsnips by peeling and cutting into quarters lengthways.
Very small parsnips may be left whole. Serve as for roast
potatoes.

BAKED POTATOES

4 large equal sized potatoes   *25 g butter*
Melted fat or cooking oil

1 Oven Gas Mark 6 or 400°F.
2 Scrub, rinse and dry potatoes. Brush over with melted fat
   or cooking oil.
3 Place on a baking tray. Prick potatoes with a fork to
   prevent skins bursting.
4 Bake for 1–2 hours, depending on the size of the potato.
   The potatoes are cooked when soft. Test by pinching.
5 Cut halfway through the potato and place butter in the
   centre of each potato.
6 Serve hot in a vegetable dish lined with a table napkin.

BAKED STUFFED POTATOES

4 large potatoes   *4 tablesp. milk*
Melted fat or oil   *Seasoning*
25 g butter   *100 g grated cheese*

1 Oven Gas Mark 6 or 400°F.
2 Prepare and cook potatoes as for baked potatoes.
3 Cut potatoes in half lengthways. Scoop out the potato, leaving skins whole.
4 Place potato into a bowl. Add butter, milk, seasoning and ⅔ of the cheese. Mix well together.
5 Refill the skins with the cheese stuffing. Smooth over the surface with a palette knife. Decorate with a fork.
6 Sprinkle remaining cheese over each half.
7 Pre-heat a grill. Grill potatoes until cheese has melted and gives a golden brown surface.
8 Serve hot in a vegetable dish lined with a table napkin.

N.B. Cheese can be substituted by other fillings:
    e.g. 100 g chopped cooked ham or bacon
         100 g cooked mushrooms or onions
         100 g skinned chopped tomatoes
         100 g cold cooked minced meat

These fillings can also be mixed:
    e.g. 50 g cheese + 50 g onions
         50 g mushrooms + 50 g bacon

CASSEROLE OF POTATOES

750 g potatoes   *125 ml milk*
25 g margarine   *Parsley for garnish*
Salt and pepper

1 Oven Gas Mark 4 or 350°F. Place margarine in a casserole dish.
2 Place in the oven to melt the fat.
3 Scrub, peel and slice potatoes 0.5 cm thick.
4 Place potatoes in the melted fat. Cover. Place in the oven to sweat for 5–10 mins.
5 Add seasoning. Boil milk in a pan and pour over the potatoes.
6 Cover with greased paper. Simmer gently in the oven for 30 mins. The potatoes are cooked when they have absorbed the milk.
7 Mash potatoes. Smooth over the surface. Decorate with a fork.

8 Serve in the same dish. Garnish with parsley.

N.B. Potatoes may be cooked in this way when a **complete** meal is cooked in the oven.

POTATO CROQUETTES }
DUCHESSE POTATOES } See Rechauffe Cookery

SAUTÉ POTATOES

250 g cooked whole potatoes   *50 g butter, margarine, dripping or cooking oil mixed with butter*

1 Slice potatoes 0.5 cm thick.
2 In a large frying pan, melt butter or margarine till bubbling, dripping until it hazes.
3 Place potato slices in the pan. Fry until golden brown on one side. Turn. Repeat until golden on both sides.
4 Drain on kitchen paper.
5 Serve immediately in a vegetable dish lined with a neat piece of kitchen paper or a napkin.

CHIPPED POTATOES

500 g potatoes   *Lard or oil for frying*
Salt

1 Prepare a deep fat frying pan and basket.
2 Scrub and peel potatoes.
3 Slice potatoes lengthways 1 cm thick. Cut each slice into lengthways strips 1 cm wide. Wash and dry well.
4 Melt lard or heat cooking oil in the deep fat frying pan. The fat or oil is ready when it browns a cube of bread in 2 mins.
5 Place chips into the basket.
6 Gently immerse the basket into the hot fat.
7 Cook until golden brown and crisp.
8 Drain on kitchen paper. Sprinkle with salt.
9 Serve as for sauté potatoes.

FRIED ONIONS

500 g onions   *50 g butter or margarine*

1 Prepare a large frying pan by melting fat in it.
2 Peel and slice the onions.
3 Heat fat in a deep fat pan.
4 Gently fry the onions in the fat until tender, transparent and golden brown.
5 Drain off excess fat.
6 Serve onions hot in a vegetable dish.

FRIED ONION RINGS

50 g S.R. flour   *2 large onions*
3 tablesp. water

1 Prepare a batter from the flour and water. (See batters. The batter should be thick enough to coat the back of a wooden spoon.)
2 Peel onion. Slice into rings.
3 Prepare a deep fat frying pan. Heat to hazing point, or piece of bread browning in 2 mins.
4 Coat onion rings in batter. Fry in deep fat until golden brown.
5 Drain on kitchen paper.
6 Serve in a vegetable dish lined with kitchen paper or on a napkin.

FRIED TOMATOES

500 g tomatoes   *25 g margarine, butter or cooking oil*

1 Blanch and skin tomatoes, cut in halves.
2 Prepare frying pan by heating oil until it browns a cube of bread in 2 mins., and the margarine or butter until it begins to bubble and forms a sediment.
3 Gently fry tomatoes in the fat about 5–6 mins. until they are thoroughly heated.
4 Drain off any excess fat.
5 Serve tomatoes and any juice in a vegetable dish.

FRIED MUSHROOMS

250 g mushrooms   *25 g margarine or butter*

1 Wash, dry and slice mushrooms. Button mushrooms may be left whole.
2 Prepare frying pan by heating margarine or butter until it begins to bubble and forms a sediment.
3 Gently fry mushrooms in the fat, about 5–6 mins., until tender and much darker in colour.
4 Drain off excess fat.
5 Serve hot in a vegetable dish.

GRILLED TOMATOES
GRILLED MUSHROOMS } See Mixed Grill

STUFFED ONIONS

4 large Spanish onions   *1 teasp. chopped parsley*
25 g white breadcrumbs   *¼ teasp. mixed herbs*
½ beaten egg   *15 g margarine*
50 g of either of the follow-   *Salt and pepper*
ing: chopped liver, ham,   *50 g margarine for cooking*
bacon, grated cheese, minced
beef or chopped mushrooms

1 Remove root and stalk. Peel the onions.
2 Place in a pan of boiling salted water. Boil for 30–45 mins. until tender.
3 Preheat oven Gas Mark 5 or 375°F.
4 Drain onions. Remove the centre of each onion, using a vegetable peeler and a spoon handle, leaving a hole about 2 cm in diameter.
5 Chop up the centre for use with the stuffing.
6 Prepare the chosen stuffing. Melt margarine, lightly fry liver, bacon, mushrooms or minced beef in the fat. Omit margarine if cheese is used. If cooked ham is used, cut margarine into small pieces and add to the breadcrumbs.
7 Add the cooked meat, mushrooms or cheese to breadcrumbs. Add chopped onion, herbs and seasonings.
8 Mix well together with the beaten egg. The stuffing should be of a stiff consistency.
9 Fill the holes with the stuffing, pressing it firmly into the centre and mounding it neatly on top.

10 Melt margarine in a roasting tin.
11 Carefully lift stuffed onions in to the tin with a fish slice. Baste the onions with the melted margarine.
12 Bake onions for about 20 mins. until slightly golden.
13 Serve with a brown sauce poured over them (see sauces).

Stuffed onions

STUFFED TOMATOES

4 large tomatoes
15 g margarine
50 g chopped liver, ham, bacon, minced beef, mushrooms or cheese
25 g white breadcrumbs
1 teasp. chopped parsley
Shallow fat for frying

$\frac{1}{4}$ teasp. mixed herbs
Seasoning
$\frac{1}{2}$ beaten egg
Margarine for cooking
4 circles of bread same size as tomatoes

1 Oven Gas Mark 4 or 350°F. Grease an oven-proof dish.
2 Wash and dry tomatoes, remove stalk.
3 Place each tomato to stand on its stalk end. Slice a circle off around the top of the tomato with a sharp pointed knife.
4 Remove juice and pips, leaving a hollow fruit. (Add these to the stuffing.)
5 Prepare stuffing as for Stuffed Onions. Stuff tomatoes.
6 Place lids aslant on the stuffing.
7 Put tomatoes closely together in the greased dish. Dot small pieces of margarine on top of each tomato.
8 Bake until they are just soft, about 30–40 mins.
9 Circles of fried bread may be prepared by cutting circles

from slices of bread with a pastry cutter. Fry in shallow fat until crisp and golden. Drain on kitchen paper.

10 Serve tomatoes arranged on top of the fried circles on an oval plate with a dish paper.

Stuffing tomatoes

STUFFED MARROW

1 medium sized marrow	*250 g cooked minced beef*
1 small onion	*Seasoning*
15 g dripping	*50 g white breadcrumbs*
15 g flour	*Dripping for cooking*
125 ml stock	

1 Peel the marrow. Cut in half lengthways. Scoop out the seeds.
2 Place marrow in a steamer, and steam until tender 30–40 mins., or boil in salted water 15–20 mins.
3 Meanwhile chop up the onion finely.
4 Melt the dripping. Lightly fry the onion in the fat. Remove onion when cooked.
5 Add the flour to the fat. Prepare a brown roux sauce with the stock (see sauces).
6 Simmer sauce for 5–10 mins., stirring all the time. Add minced beef. Season to taste.
7 Add breadcrumbs to beef mixture to stiffen.
8 Remove marrow from steamer when tender.
9 Preheat oven Gas Mark 5 or 375°F. Place dripping to melt in a roasting tin.
10 Stuff each half of the marrow with the filling. Sandwich together so that both edges meet.
11 Carefully lay into roasting tin. Baste all over.
12 Bake for 20 mins.

13 Serve hot in an oval dish with brown sauce served around it.

Stuffing marrow

11

Hot and cold sweets

(See also Section on Batters)

BAKED APPLES

*To each cooking apple
25 g dried fruit, e.g.
cherries, sultanas, currants
dates or nuts or a mixture*

*1 tablesp. golden syrup or
demerara sugar*

1 Oven 350°F/Gas Mark 4. Put 2 cm depth water in a pie or
casserole dish.
2 Wash the apples. Remove the cores with a corer or
vegetable peeler.
3 Cut a slit all the way round through the skin $\frac{2}{3}$ of the way
up the apples to prevent them bursting.
4 Stand apples in the dish. Mix the filling ingredients. Stuff
the centres of the apples with the mixture.

Stuffing apples

5 Cook 20–40 mins. till the apples feel soft and fluffy. Over-cooking will make the apples collapse.
6 Serve with custard.

N.B. If liked, fruit may be omitted and the syrup merely poured over the apples.

APPLE CHARLOTTE

500 g cooking apples
1–2 tablesp. cold water
100 g sugar

Zest and juice of half a lemon
60 g margarine
4–6 thin slices bread (crusts removed)

1 Oven 400°F/Gas Mark 6.
2 Peel, core and cut the apples into pieces, stew in the water and sugar in a pan with a tightly fitting lid, till soft, about 10 mins.
3 Add the finely grated lemon zest and juice.
4 Melt the margarine. Cut the bread into lengths, dip it in the margarine to coat completely, and line the sides and bottom of a pie dish. (Save some for the top.)
5 Pour in the apples. Cover the top with the rest of the dipped bread.
6 Cook 30–45 mins. until brown and crisp. Sprinkle with sugar, serve hot with custard.

N.B. Breadcrumbs may be used instead of bread, put in layers with the apples.

MILK PUDDING

Whole or medium grain

15 g margarine
50 g Carolina rice, sago, tapioca or macaroni
500 ml milk

A pinch of salt
50 g sugar
Grated nutmeg

1 Oven 300°F/Gas Mark 2. Grease a 500 ml pie dish with the margarine. Stand it on a baking sheet.
2 Wash the grain in a sieve.
3 Put into the pie dish, add the milk, salt and sugar.
4 Sprinkle nutmeg on top.
5 Bake 1½–2 hrs. till beginning to thicken.

N.B. An egg may be added to enrich the pudding. Stewed fruit may be served with it.

Ground Grain—e.g. semolina and Ground Rice

500 ml milk	*50 g sugar*
50 g grain semolina or ground rice	*1 egg if liked*

1 Oven 325°F/Gas Mark 3. Grease a pie dish. Stand it on a baking sheet.
2 Warm the milk, sprinkle in the grain, stir until boiling, cook 5 mins., add the sugar, cool if egg is to be used.
3 Beat in the egg. Pour into the pie dish.
4 Cook 20–30 mins. till creamy.

MOULDS

50 g cornflour	*Flavouring and colouring*
50 g sugar	*e.g. vanilla essence, grated*
500 ml milk	*lemon zest, 2 teasp. cocoa or 1 tablesp. coffee essence*

1 Wet a mould or basin (500 ml size).
2 Blend the cornflour and sugar to a thin paste with a little of the milk, adding cocoa if used.
3 Boil the rest of the milk. Pour on to the cornflour, stirring. Return to the rinsed pan. Bring to the boil, cook 2–3 mins., stirring. Add the flavouring and colourings.
4 Pour into the mould, cover with damp greaseproof paper. Leave to set. Loosen and turn out. Serve with stewed fruit.

BREAD AND BUTTER PUDDING

50 g margarine	*Grated zest of 1 lemon*
4 slices of stale bread (crusts may be removed)	*500 ml milk*
100 g dried fruit	*50 g granulated sugar*
2 eggs	*25 g demerara sugar*

1 Oven 350°F/Gas Mark 4. Grease a pie dish, stand it on a baking sheet.
2 Spread the margarine on the bread, cut into triangles.
3 Put the bread and fruit in layers in a dish.
4 Beat the eggs, add the milk, granulated sugar and lemon zest if used. Strain into the dish. Leave to soak 30 mins.
5 Sprinkle the demerara sugar on top. Cook 30–40 mins. till set.

BAKED EGG CUSTARD

500 ml milk
2–3 eggs
50 g sugar
Grated nutmeg

1 Oven 325°F/Gas Mark 3.
2 Warm the milk, beat the eggs, add the sugar, pour on the milk.
3 Strain into a pie dish. Leave to stand 10 mins. to remove air bubbles.
4 Sprinkle nutmeg on top. Stand dish in a bain marie. Cook 1 hour till just firm to the touch. Serve hot or cold with fruit.

FRUIT CRUMBLE

100 g S.R. flour
50 g margarine
100 g sugar—50 g for the fruit
500 g fruit, e.g. apples, black-berries, gooseberries

1 Oven 375°F/Gas Mark 5. Put a pie dish on a baking sheet.
2 Put the flour, margarine and half the sugar in a bowl. Rub in till like golden breadcrumbs.
3 Wash and prepare the fruit according to kind. Put half into the dish, add the remaining sugar, then the other half of the fruit.
4 Sprinkle the crumble mixture on top, do not press down. Level off with a palette knife. Wipe the edge of the dish. Cook 45 mins. till the crumble is golden brown and the fruit is tender (it will sing when done).
5 Serve hot with custard or cream.

STEAMED RUBBED-IN PUDDING

optional flavouring of 2 tab-lesp. syrup or jam or mar-malade placed in the bottom of the basin
75 g margarine
150 g S.R. flour
75 g sugar
100 g dried fruit
Grated zest of orange or lemon
1 egg
Milk to mix

For a chocolate pudding, remove a rounded tablesp. flour, add one of cocoa.

1 Put a steamer on to boil. Grease a pudding basin (put jam

or syrup in the bottom, if used), and a piece of grease-proof paper or foil.

2 Rub the margarine into the flour and sugar until like golden breadcrumbs.

3 Add the flavourings, beaten egg and enough milk to make a dropping consistency.

4 Put into the basin, cover with foil or paper, greased side down.

5 Steam 1–1½ hrs. till spongy and skewer comes out clean. Turn out. Serve with custard or jam sauce.

Suet Puddings

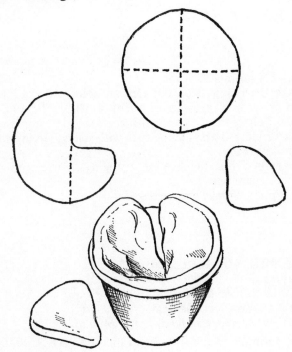

Lining a basin with suet pastry

FRUIT DUMPLINGS

150 g suet pastry   500 g fruit—apples,
75 g sugar   rhubarb, gooseberries

1 Put on the steamer. Grease a pudding basin and a piece of greaseproof or foil.

2 Make the suet pastry (see pastries). Take ⅔ of the pastry, roll into a circle and use to line the basin, press towards the top with the fingers.
3 Prepare and slice the fruit, put into the pastry with the sugar. Damp the edges of the pastry. Roll out the last ⅓ to form a lid, place on the fruit, seal. Cover with paper or foil.
4 Steam 1½–2 hrs. Turn out. Serve with a sweet white sauce or custard.

JAM ROLY POLY

150 g suet pastry (see pastries)   *3 tablesp. jam or syrup*
or 50 g currants or sultanas

1 Put on a steamer.
2 Make the pastry. Roll out into an oblong. Spread with jam or syrup or sprinkle with fruit to within 2 cm of the edge. Roll up firmly, cover with greased greaseproof paper or a pudding cloth. Tie the ends with string, leaving some room for rising.
3 Steam 1½–2 hrs. Remove the wrappings. Serve with custard or a jam sauce.
This pudding may also be baked.

STEAMED SUET PUDDING

150 g S.R. flour and bread-   *75 g sugar*
crumbs mixed together in   *75 g suet*
equal quantities, or all flour   *Milk to mix*

Flavourings—to the foundation mixture may be added ½ teasp. mixed spice or 2 tablesp. syrup and 1 teasp. ginger added to the mixture, or 2 tablesp. syrup and 50 g dried fruit.

1 Put on a steamer. Grease a 500 ml pudding basin and a piece of greaseproof paper or foil.
2 Mix flour, sugar, suet and breadcrumbs and add milk to make a soft paste. Add flavourings. Place in a basin. Cover.
3 Steam 1½–2 hrs. Turn out. Serve with a sauce, e.g. custard, syrup sauce.

CHRISTMAS PUDDING

100 g plain flour   *100 g demerara sugar*
100 g suet   *Pinch grated nutmeg*
½ teasp. mixed spice   *25g blanched chopped almonds*
375 g mixed dried fruit and *Grated zest and juice, half a*
peel   *lemon*
50 g breadcrumbs   *3 eggs*

1 Put on a steamer. Grease a large basin and a piece of foil or greaseproof paper.
2 Mix dry ingredients. Add beaten eggs and lemon juice to make a stiff consistency. Place in basin. Cover.
3 Steam 8–12 hrs. till dark. Cool, re-cover. Leave to mature in a dry place.
   Inspect every week. On Christmas Day steam 2 hrs. Serve with a sweet white sauce or brandy or rum butter.

For **CREAMED RICH CAKE MIXTURE PUDDINGS,** see creamed cake mixtures.

STEAMED PUDDING

75–100 g margarine   *Flavourings as for a rubbed-*
75–100 g caster sugar   *in steamed pudding*
2 eggs   *Milk to mix*
150 g S.R. flour

Castle puddings may be made by dividing the mixture into 4–5 greased dariole moulds with jam in the bottom and steaming ¾ hr.

1 Put on a steamer. Grease a pudding basin and a piece of foil or greaseproof paper.
2 Cream margarine and sugar, beat in eggs a little at a time.
3 Fold in flour and flavouring, adding milk to make dropping consistency. Put into basin. Cover.
4 Steam 1½–2 hrs. Turn out. Serve with a sauce e.g. jam or custard.

EVE'S PUDDING

500 g apples, rhubarb or goose- *50 g caster sugar*
berries   *1 egg*

1-2 tablesp. water   100 g S.R. flour
50 g granulated sugar   Milk to mix
50 g margarine

1 Oven 350°F/Gas Mark 4. Grease a pie dish.
2 Prepare and stew fruit with water and granulated sugar in a closed pan till soft.
3 Cream margarine and caster sugar, gradually beat in egg, fold in flour. Add milk to make a dropping consistency.
4 Put apples in the dish. Smooth cake mixture over.
5 Cook 40–45 mins. till risen and golden and springs back when pressed.
Serve with custard.

UPSIDE-DOWN PUDDING OR CAKE

2 tablesp. syrup or 50 g margarine and 50g demerara sugar
Pineapple rings or oranges or peaches or pears, etc.
Glacé cherries for decoration

50 g margarine
50 g caster sugar
1 egg
100 g S.R. flour
Milk to mix

1 Oven 350°F/Gas Mark 4.
2 Line the bottom and sides of a round pie dish or 16 cm cake tin with syrup or creamed margarine and demerara sugar. Drain the fruit, arrange good side down in the dish.
3 Cream margarine and sugar. Beat in egg, gradually. Fold in the flour, add milk to make a soft dropping consistency.
4 Spread carefully over the fruit. Cook 40 mins. till golden brown, risen and springs back when pressed. Turn on to a plate. Serve hot with an arrowroot syrup sauce or cold with cream. Decorate with glacé cherries.

N.B. A chocolate cake can be made by taking 1 level tablesp. flour from the weighed quantity and adding one of cocoa.

BAKED JAM SPONGE

3 tablesp. jam   *1 egg*
50 g margarine   *100 g S.R. flour*
50 g caster sugar   *Milk to mix*

1 Oven 350°F/Gas Mark 4. Grease a pie dish.
2 Spread jam in the bottom of a pie dish.
3 Cream margarine and sugar. Gradually beat in egg, fold

in flour, add milk to make a dropping consistency. Spread over the jam.
4 Bake 35–40 mins. till springs back when pressed. Serve with custard.

COUNTESS PUDDING

Use the above recipe using syrup instead of jam and adding 50 g currants to the mixture with the flour.

APPLE DUMPLINGS OR BALLS

To each medium cooking apple
50 g short crust pastry
1 tablesp. brown sugar

¼ teasp. ground cloves or lemon rind or cinnamon (optional)
A little caster sugar

1 Oven 400°F/Gas Mark 6. Grease a baking sheet.
2 Make the pastry. Divide into equal sized pieces, one for each apple.
3 Knead the pieces to rounds and roll them out, 2 cm larger all round than the apples.
4 Peel the apples, remove the core, put on the pastry with the flatter side down. Fill with brown sugar and the chosen flavouring mixed together.
5 Shape the pastry up round the apple, pressing out all creases. Damp the pastry edges and press together.
6 Turn the balls over, brush with water, dredge with caster sugar.
7 Cook 15 mins. then reduce the heat and cook 30 mins. at 325°F/Gas Mark 3 until the pastry is crisp and golden.
Serve on a round plate with custard.

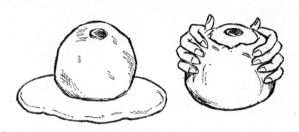

Apple balls or dumplings

FRUIT TART

250 g short crust pastry   2–3 tablesp. sugar
375–500 g fruit, e.g.
apples, plums, gooseberries,
bilberries

1 Oven 400°F/Gas Mark 6.
2 Make the pastry (see pastries). Divide into 2 pieces, one slightly smaller than the other.
3 Use the smaller of the two pieces to line a 16 cm over-proof plate. Damp the edge of the pastry.
4 Prepare the fruit, according to kind. Place on the pastry, adding sugar.
5 Roll out the second piece of pastry large enough to cover the plate and fruit. Use to cover the tart. Seal and decorate the edges.
6 Cut two slits in the top to allow the steam to escape. Cook 25–30 mins. till the pastry is golden brown and the fruit is soft (boiling and singing).
7 Dredge with caster sugar. Serve hot with custard, cold with cream.

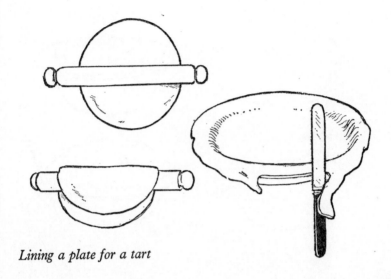

Lining a plate for a tart

FRUIT PIE

150 g short crust pastry   *50–100 g sugar*
500 g fruit, e.g. plums,   *A little water if the fruit is*
apples, rhubarb, gooseberries,   *hard*
etc.

1 Oven 400°F/Gas Mark 6.
2 Make the pastry (see pastries).
3 Prepare the fruit according to kind. Place in the dish. The
  fruit must come into a mound above the sides of the dish
  or the pastry will collapse. Add the sugar, and water if
  used.
4 Roll out the pastry 2 cm larger than the pie dish all round.
  (Stand dish on pastry to measure). Cut off 2 cm of the
  pastry on all sides. Damp the edge of the dish and use the
  trimmings to line the dish edge.
5 Damp the strips. Place on the lid, seal and decorate the
  edge.
6 Place on a baking sheet. Cook about 30 mins. till the
  pastry is golden and the fruit is soft. (The fruit will boil
  and sing).
7 Dredge the top of the pie with caster sugar. Serve with
  custard or cream.

Covering a pie

Pastry leaves and tassel

PLATE JAM TART

100–120 g short crust pastry   *2 tablesp. jam or lemon curd or mincemeat*

1 Oven 400°F/Gas Mark 6.
2 Make the pastry (see pastries). Line an ovenproof 16 cm plate. Trim and decorate the edge. Spread jam or lemon curd or mincemeat on the well in the pastry. Decorate with strips of pastry to make a lattice, twists of pastry, leaves, etc.
3 Cook 20 mins. till the pastry is golden. Serve with custard or cream.

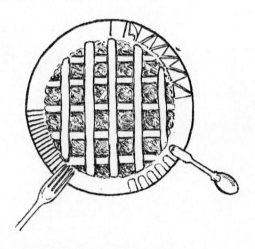

Lattice jam tart—varieties of edging

TREACLE TART

100 g short crust pastry   *3–4 tablesp. syrup*
3–4 tablesp. bread or cake   *Grated zest and juice of*
crumbs or rolled oats or $\frac{1}{4}$ *lemon*
crushed cornflakes   *Pinch of ground ginger, optional*

1 Oven 425°F/Gas Mark 7.
2 Make the pastry. Line a 16 cm oven-proof plate.
3 Mix the other ingredients and finish as for plate jam tart.

LEMON MERINGUE PIE

100 g short crust pastry
25 g cornflour
125 ml water
30 g sugar to each lemon

15 g butter or margarine
2 egg yolks
Finely grated zest and juice of
2 small or 1 large lemon
Meringue: 2 egg whites
100 g caster sugar

1 Oven 400°F/Gas Mark 6.
2 Make the pastry (see pastries). Use to line a 14 cm fluted flan ring. Bake blind 20 mins. till set.
3 Blend together the cornflour, finely grated zest of lemon and the water. Boil well, stirring all the time. Add the sugar, lemon juice and margarine.
4 Cool. Add the yolks to the mixture. Pour into the flan case.
5 Whisk the egg whites till stiff. Gradually whisk in $\frac{1}{2}$ the sugar till the whites are again stiff. Fold in the rest.
6 Pile on to the flan. If serving hot, flash cook 10–15 mins. at 425°F/Gas Mark 7, or if serving cold dry out in a cool oven 250°–275°F or Gas Mark $\frac{1}{2}$ until crisp, about $1\frac{1}{2}$–2 hrs.

APPLE AMBER

100 g short crust pastry
25 g margarine
2 egg yolks
1 tablesp. water
Meringue:
2 egg whites
100 g caster sugar

Zest of half a lemon and a
little juice
500 g apples
2 tablesp. sugar

1 Oven 375°F/Gas Mark 5.
2 Prepare and stew the apples with the water and sugar, rub through a sieve.
3 Make the pastry. Use to line a pie dish and prick.
4 Melt the margarine and add to the apples with the finely grated zest and juice of the lemon.
5 Separate the eggs, adding the yolks to the apples. Pour into the pastry. Cook 30–45 mins. till the pastry is cooked and the mixture is set.
6 Whisk the whites till stiff. Gradually whisk in half the caster sugar till stiff. Fold in the rest. Pile on to the apples. Cook 10–15 mins. till golden. Serve hot.

BAKEWELL TART

100 g short crust pastry or   *50 g margarine*
flan crust   *1 egg*
50 g caster sugar   *25 g cake crumbs (trifle*
50 g ground almonds   *sponge cake)*
Few drops almond essence   *Glacé icing and glacé cherries*
1–2 tablesp. jam, usually   *for decoration if liked*
raspberry

1 Oven 350°F/Gas Mark 4.
2 Make the pastry (see pastry), line a 14 cm flan ring or pie plate, prick.
3 Spread with jam.
4 Make the filling by the creaming method (see cake mixtures). Spread onto the jam.
5 Cook 40–45 mins. till golden and set.
6 When cold the top may be iced with white glace icing and decorated with glacé cherries.

QUEEN OF PUDDINGS

500 ml milk   *50 g sugar*
100 g bread or cake crumbs   *2 eggs*
100 g caster sugar   *Finely grated zest of 1 lemon*
3 tablesp. jam   *Glacé cherries and angelica*
50 g margarine   *for decoration*

1 Oven 325°F/Gas Mark 3.
2 Heat the margarine and milk together and pour over the breadcrumbs. Add half the sugar.
3 Separate the eggs. Add the yolks to the mixture and the finely grated zest of the lemon.
4 Allow to stand 30 mins. or longer. Pour into a pie dish and bake till firm and set, about 25 mins.
5 Remove from the oven. Spread with jam.
6 Whisk the whites till stiff. Gradually whisk in half the caster sugar till the whites are again stiff, fold in the rest. Pile on the jam. Cook 5–10 mins. at 425°F or Gas Mark 7 till golden brown. Decorate with glacé cherries and angelica.

MANCHESTER TART

100 g short crust pastry

2 bananas
Jam
250 ml thick custard
(1 rounded tablesp. custard
powder, 1 rounded tablesp.
sugar)
Coconut or glace cherries for
decoration

1 Oven 400°F/Gas Mark 6.
2 Make the pastry (see pastries). Line a 14 cm flan ring or sandwich tin. Bake blind 20 mins. till firm, cool.
3 Spread the jam on the pastry. Slice the bananas and arrange on the jam in layers.
4 Make the custard, cool and spread on to the tart.
5 Decorate with coconut or glacé cherries.

BANANA AND ORANGE MERINGUE

2 bananas   *Meringue:*
2 oranges   *2 egg whites*
50 g granulated sugar   *100 g caster sugar*

1 Oven 300°F/Gas Mark 2 or 425°F/Gas Mark 7.
2 Slice the bananas lengthways and cut in half. Segment oranges. Place in an oven-proof dish, sprinkle with granulated sugar.
3 Whisk egg whites till stiff. Gradually whisk in half the caster sugar, fold in the other half. Pile on to the fruit and either dry out 2 hrs. in a cool oven, serve cold, or flash cook, 10–15 mins. and serve hot.

Cold Sweets

STEWED FRUIT

500 g fruit, e.g. apples,   2 tablesp. sugar
rhubarb, gooseberries, pears,   2 tablesp. water
plums, etc.

(For fruit with skins e.g. plums, gooseberries, more water may be needed and longer cooking)
1 Prepare the fruit, remove cores, etc., cutting up rhubarb into chunks.

2 Put all ingredients in a saucepan, cover, simmer till tender and not broken. (10 mins. apples, 20–30 mins. gooseberries).

To stew in the oven put the fruit and sugar in a casserole. Boil the water and add. Cook in the bottom of a moderate oven 350°F/Gas Mark 4, 20–30 mins. till tender.

FRUIT FOOL

500 g fruit, e.g. gooseberries, raspberries, apples, blackberries, bilberries, rhubarb
2 tablesp. water
2 tablesp. sugar
(more water may be required for hard fruit)

Custard:
250 ml milk
1 level tablesp. sugar
Colouring as required
1 level tablesp. custard powder
125 ml custard and 125 ml cream or evaporated milk may be used instead of all custard

1 Wash the fruit. Remove skin, cores, etc. Chop. Place in a saucepan with the water and sugar, cover, stew until tender.
2 Rub through a sieve.
3 Make the custard by the blending method (see sauces), cool. Whip the cream or evaporated milk if used.
4 Add to the fruit purée, colour if necessary. Pour into individual bowls or one large dish. Serve with cream, biscuits or sponge fingers. Chopped nuts may be sprinkled on the surface.

N.B. Banana fool may be made by rubbing fresh bananas through a sieve and combining with the custard etc.

FRESH FRUIT SALAD

250 ml water
4 rounded tablesp. sugar
1 lemon

Tinned fruit may be added to give colour when necessary, e.g. cherries.

500 g fresh fruit in season, e.g. dessert apples, peaches, orange, grapefruit, bananas, grapes, strawberries, cherries, pineapple, melon, pears, apricots, raspberries

1 Put water and sugar in a saucepan. Peel the zest from the lemon and orange, add. Boil 5–8 mins., strain and cool. Wash fruit.

2 Leave apples, pears and bananas till last as they turn brown. To help prevent this, place in lemon juice immediately after cutting. Peaches also should be dipped in lemon juice, for the same reason.

3 Remove orange and grapefruit segments from skin, core and slice apples and pears. Cut all fruit into even sized pieces, half grapes, etc.

4 Apple and pear skin may be left on to add colour.

5 Pour the syrup over the fruit. Serve in individual dishes or an attractive large glass dish. Serve immediately with cream or ice cream.

(For more detailed preparation of fruit, see page 192).

Peeling an orange

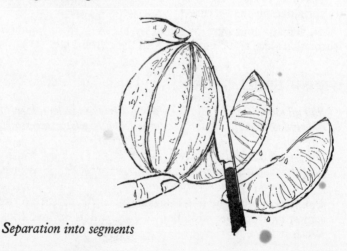

Separation into segments

APPLE SNOW

500 g apples
2 tablesp. water
2 eggs, separated
zest of 1 lemon

75–120 g sugar
3 or 4 sponge cakes or stale
cake
250 ml milk
15 g sugar

1 Peel, core, chop the apples, stew with water, finely grated lemon zest and most of the sugar in a covered pan till tender. Sieve.
2 Slice the sponge cakes into a glass dish.
3 Make the custard by placing yolks, milk and the remaining 15 g sugar in a bowl over hot water and cooking slowly, stirring till it thickens (about 20 mins.).
(Custard powder may be used instead)
4 Pour the custard over the cakes.
5 Whisk the whites stiffly, gradually add the fruit purée, whisking until stiff.
6 Pile the whisked mixture on to the custard.

TRIFLE

4 sponge cakes or stale cake
1 tablesp. jam
125 ml fruit syrup or sherry
Tin of fruit optional
Nuts, cherries, ratafia biscuits, angelica etc. for decoration

250 ml thick custard
125–150 ml double cream

1 Split the sponge cakes, spread with jam. Cut into small pieces.
2 Place in a glass dish or individual dishes. Drain the fruit if used. Pour the syrup or sherry over the cakes and leave to soak.
3 Add the fruit if used. Make the custard, pour over the sponge cakes. Leave till cold.
4 Whip the cream, spread or pipe on to the trifle. Decorate with ratafia biscuits, nuts, cherries or angelica.

EGG CUSTARD TART

100 g short crust pastry
2 eggs
nutmeg

250 ml milk
25 g sugar

1 Oven 400°F/Gas Mark 6.
2 Make the pastry (see pastries). Use to line a flan ring or 14 cm sandwich tin. Press the pastry well down to remove air and avoid making holes in the pastry or the custard will leak through and the pastry rise.
3 Warm the milk. Beat the eggs and sugar. Pour the milk on to them. Strain into the pastry. Leave to stand to remove air. Sprinkle with grated nutmeg.
4 Cook 25 mins. (reduce heat to 350°F/Gas Mark 4 after 10 mins.) till golden and the custard is set. Cool. Serve on a plate with a doyley, middle removed.

DATE CUSTARD TART

As for baked egg custard, adding 12 dates to the custard.

COLD SOUFFLÉ (Lemon)

2 eggs
50 g caster sugar
zest and juice of 1 lemon

2 tablesp. water
125 ml double cream or evaporated milk
2 level teasp. gelatin (10 g)

To decorate: angelica, cherries, nuts, whipped cream

1 Tie a double band of greaseproof paper around a soufflé dish (250 ml) so that it stands 6 cm above the rim of the dish or use a larger dish and omit the greaseproof.
2 Separate the eggs. Put the yolks and sugar in a bowl. Grate the lemon zest finely and add with the juice to the yolks.
3 Whisk over hot water until thick. (Do not overheat).
4 Remove from the heat, whisk until cold.
5 Dissolve the gelatin in cold water in a basin standing in a saucepan of hot water.
6 Pour the gelatin from a height and fold into the yolk mixture.
7 Whisk the cream or evaporated milk till thick.
8 Using a clean, dry grease-free whisk, beat the egg whites till stiff.
9 Fold cream and whites into the yolk mixture, pour into the case. Leave to set in a cool place. Do not leave too long in a refrigerator or the gelatin becomes tough.
10 Remove greaseproof by holding the back of a knife flat against the greaseproof paper, pulling the paper round it, thus leaving a smooth edge to the soufflé. Decorate.

ORANGE SOUFFLÉ
rind and juice of one orange instead of lemon.

CHOCOLATE SOUFFLÉ

50 g chocolate   *2–3 drops vanilla essence*
2 tablesp. water

Grate the chocolate and melt with the water in a basin over hot water, add the yolks, sugar and vanilla essence. Proceed as before.

CHOCOLATE MOUSSE

4 eggs   *Knob of butter*
100 g plain chocolate grated *Vanilla essence*
2 tablesp. sugar   *Chocolate and nuts for*
                               decoration

1 Separate the eggs.
2 Put the grated chocolate, sugar, yolks, butter, vanilla essence, in a basin over a saucepan of hot water. Melt slowly, stirring till thick. Do not overheat. Cool.
3 Whisk the whites and fold into the mixture.
4 Pour into individual glasses, chill, decorate with grated chocolate or nuts.

FRUIT FLAN

100 g short crust pastry or flan crust pastry
1 medium tin fruit, e.g. cherries, oranges, pineapple
125 ml fruit syrup
1 heaped teasp. arrowroot or cornflour

OR fresh fruit, e.g. strawberries and 125 ml sugar syrup made by boiling water and sugar together in a saucepan (250 ml water, 100 g sugar). Measure 125 ml from this. This may be coloured
Cherries and angelica for decoration

1 Oven 400°F/Gas Mark 6.
2 Make the pastry, line a flan ring. Bake blind 20–25 mins. till golden. Cool.
3 Drain the fruit well. Arrange in the flan ring.
4 Blend the arrowroot and syrup. Bring to the boil, stirring,

and boil 2–3 mins. till clear and it coats the spoon. Cool a little then spoon over the fruit. Leave to set. Decorate with cherries and angelica.
Serve on a doyley, middle removed.

FRUIT CONDÉ

Flavouring—drop of vanilla essence or 1 teasp. grated orange or lemon rind
2 tablesp. cream or evaporated milk (optional)

250 ml rice pudding (see the rice pudding recipe) or a tin of rice pudding
Fruit—tinned pears or peaches or apricots
4 tablesp. jam for glaze, apricot, raspberry, etc.

1 Add flavouring and cream to the rice. Place in a glass dish.
2 Put the fruit on top.
3 Warm the jam, sieve, pour over the fruit.

ORANGE SNOW

1 large tin evaporated milk
50 g caster sugar
Zest and juice of one orange

15 g gelatin
2 tablesp. water
Juice ½ lemon

N.B. All lemons may be used.
1 Whisk evaporated milk and sugar till thick and creamy. Fold in juice and zest.
2 Dissolve gelatin in water by warming over a pan of hot water. Pour, fold into the mixture. Leave to cool.

12

Réchauffé cookery

Rules for using leftovers
1 All foods should be as fresh as possible.
2 Mince, chop and divide foods before use.
3 Add moisture in the form of a sauce or gravy.
4 Reheat, do not recook.
5 Add extra seasonings or flavouring by using strong flavoured vegetables, e.g. onions.
6 Reheat thoroughly.
7 Serve as attractively as possible. Vary colours and texture.
8 Serve a food rich in Vitamin C with the reheated dish.
9 Do not reheat more than once.

FISH CAKES

250 g cooked fish or canned salmon, pilchards, etc.
250 g cooked potato
Seasoning
½ teasp. lemon juice
125 ml binding white sauce,
(i.e. 125 ml milk, 1 rounded tablesp. cornflour) or beaten egg
Raspings and beaten egg for coating
Parsley for garnish

1 Remove bones and skin from cooked fish.
2 Flake and mash fish on a plate.
3 Mash the potato, add the fish, beat till smooth.
4 Season, add lemon juice and enough sauce or beaten egg to make it possible to shape the mixture.
5 On a floured surface, form the mixture into a long roll and cut into 8–10 cakes. Neaten the shape of the cakes.
6 Coat with egg and raspings. Beat the egg on a plate, put the raspings on a piece of greaseproof, brush each cake with egg, shake in the crumbs. Repeat.
7 Fry in shallow fat that browns bread in 20 secs. Turn once, drain. Serve on a hot oval plate garnished with

parsley. Serve a sauce and vegetables to complete the meal.

FISH PIE

500 g cooked fish	*Seasoning*
500 g cooked potato	*1 tablesp. grated cheese or*
Parsley for garnish	*sliced tomato*

1 Flake the fish, remove bones.
2 Mix with potato, season.
3 Place in a pie dish, smooth over. Cover with grated cheese or slices of tomato.
4 Grill or heat through in an oven to brown. Garnish with parsley, serve with a sauce, e.g. parsley or egg.

RUSSIAN FISH PIE

200 g rough puff or flaky pastry (see pastries)	*125 ml white or coating parsley sauce*
250 g cooked fish	*Beaten egg for glazing*
Seasoning	*1 hard boiled egg*
	Parsley for garnish

1 Oven 425°F/Gas Mark 7.
2 Make the pastry.
3 Flake the fish, add seasoning, sauce, chopped hard boiled egg and allow to cool.
4 Roll out the pastry into a 30 cm square. Trim the edges and roll the trimmings to make four long leaves.
5 Pile the fish mixture in the middle of the pastry. Arrange sliced hard boiled egg on top.
6 Damp the edges of the pastry with egg and fold the square to an envelope shape, overlapping the edges 1 cm.
7 Brush with beaten egg and make a hole in the top to allow the steam to escape. Arrange the leaves to cover the joins. Brush them with egg.
8 Bake 30–40 mins. till golden brown. Serve on an oval dish garnished with parsley.

SHEPHERD'S PIE

Make as for Shepherd's pie in the meat section but use leftover, cooked, minced meat.

RISSOLES OR MEAT CROQUETTES

250 g cooked meat or chicken   *Seasoning*
125 ml binding white sauce   *Egg and raspings for coating*
Parsley for garnish

1 Mince meat, make the sauce.
2 Mix together, add seasoning.
3 Cool, divide into 8 portions and make into flat cakes or cork-shaped pieces.
4 Egg and crumb and fry as for fish cakes. Croquettes may be fried in deep fat. Drain.
5 Serve on an oval plate, garnished with parsley.

MEAT PASTIES

Make as for Cornish pasties in the meat section, using left-over cooked meat.

POTATO CROQUETTES

500 g cooked potato   *Seasoning*
15 g butter or margarine   *Beaten egg, raspings, for*
Parsley for garnish   *coating*

1 Mash and beat potatoes till smooth, adding butter and seasoning. (The potatoes may be sieved.)
2 Form into balls or croquette shapes on a floured board.
3 Egg and crumb as for fish cakes.
4 Fry in deep fat till golden brown. Drain. Garnish with parsley, serve on an oval plate or in a tureen.

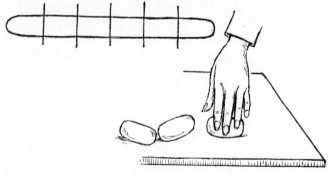

Croquette potatoes—rolling and shaping

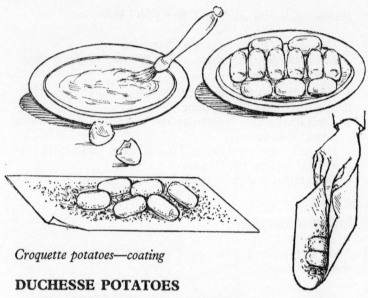

Croquette potatoes—coating

DUCHESSE POTATOES

500 g cooked potatoes   Seasoning
15 g margarine   Grated nutmeg
1 beaten egg   A little milk if necessary

1 Oven 400°F/Gas Mark 6. Grease a baking sheet. Sieve potatoes.
2 Add margarine (melted if the potatoes are cold), add the egg. Beat well, add seasoning and a pinch of nutmeg. To make a smooth consistency from a dry mixture, a little milk may be added.
3 Put the mixture into a large forcing bag fitted with a star savoy tube.
4 Pipe rosettes or stars on the baking sheet. Leave to set and dry out in an oven for 10 mins. Brush with beaten egg.
5 Heat and brown till crisp on the surface, 15–20 mins. Serve on an oval plate, garnished with parsley. Duchesse potato may be used to line the edge of a dish of meat or fish, etc.

VEGETABLE FLAN

100 g short crust pastry
125 ml coating cheese sauce
150 g cooked vegetables, e.g.
peas, beans, carrots, onions,
etc.

Seasoning
Parsley for garnish

1 Oven 400°F/Gas Mark 6.
2 Line a flan ring with the pastry, prick. Bake blind 20–25 mins. till firm.
3 Make the cheese sauce, add the vegetables and seasoning. Pour into the flan case. Serve hot or cold garnished with neat slices of vegetables or with parsley.

EGG AND BACON PIE

250 g mashed potatoes
3 tablesp. milk
2 rashers bacon
Parsley for garnish

25 g margarine
Seasoning
2 eggs

1 Oven 375°F/Gas Mark 5. Grease a large pie dish.
2 Put the mashed potatoes, margarine and 2 tablesp. of milk into a pan. Heat and beat till smooth. Season.
3 Pile into the dish, smooth. Bake 20 mins. till golden.
4 Fry the bacon (do not crisp), chop. Pour the fat left from frying over the potato mixture, sprinkle the bacon on top.
5 Beat the eggs with 1 tablesp. of remaining milk. Season. Pour over the bacon.
6 Bake in the same oven till set. Serve garnished with parsley.

RISOTTO

25 g lard
1 chopped onion (small)
250 g patna rice
500 ml stock
Seasoning

100 g chopped cooked meat or poultry
100 g chopped cooked mushrooms
Parmesan cheese grated (optional)

1 In a heavy frying pan melt the lard and dice and fry the chopped onion, slowly, till tender.
2 Add the unwashed rice, fry 3 mins.

3 Add one third of the stock, bring to the boil, cook 20 mins. till the rice is tender, adding the remaining stock gradually as required. Stir as little as possible.
4 Season, add the cooked meat and mushrooms, heat.
5 Pile into dish. Serve with grated cheese.

N.B. Tinned tomatoes may be substituted for the stock and other ingredients, egg, sultanas, chopped blanched tomato may be added.

CHEESE AND POTATO CAKES

1 onion   *100 g cheese*
Seasoning   *500 g mashed potato*
Parsley for garnish   *Egg and raspings for coating*

1 Peel and boil onion in salted water till tender. Drain, chop.
2 Grate the cheese, mix with the potatoes, onion and seasoning. Form into cakes or croquette shapes on a floured board. Coat as for fish cakes.
3 Fry in deep fat that browns bread in 2 mins., until golden, drain.
4 Serve on a hot oval dish, garnished with parsley.

CHICKEN RISSOLES

1 cooked onion   *1 chicken stock cube for seas-*
500 g cooked potato   *oning*
250 g cooked minced chicken *Raspings and beaten egg for*
                                               coating
                                               Parsley for garnish

1 Chop onion, mash potatoes, add to minced chicken.
2 Crumble stock cube into mixture. Mix well.
3 Divide into 6–8 portions. Shape into round flat cakes about 2 cm thick.
4 Coat twice in egg and breadcrumbs.
5 Fry in deep fat, which browns bread in 2 mins., until golden brown and crisp. Drain.
6 Serve on a hot oval dish. Garnish with parsley.

N.B. The rissoles can also be fried in shallow fat, turning once.

13
Cakes, biscuits and icings

Rubbing-in method of cake making

Plain cakes

ROCK BUNS

100 g S.R. flour   *50 g currants or sultanas*
50 g margarine   *½ beaten egg*
50 g sugar

1 Oven 400°F/Gas Mark 6. Grease a baking tray.
2 Sieve flour into a mixing bowl.
3 Rub fat into flour until like breadcrumbs.
4 Add sugar and fruit.
5 Mix to a stiff consistency with beaten egg.
6 Pile into 8–10 rocky heaps.
7 Bake for 15–20 mins. Test by pressing lightly in the centre. If the mixture springs back, the cakes are cooked. Cool on a wire tray.
8 Serve on a round plate with a doyley.

N.B. Cherry and coconut buns may be made in exactly the same way by substituting for the fruit 50 g chopped glacé cherries or 50 g desiccated coconut.

JAM BUNS

100 g S.R. flour   *½ beaten egg*
50 g margarine   *Raspberry jam*
50 g sugar

1 Oven 400°F/Gas Mark 6. Grease baking tray.

2 Sieve flour into a mixing bowl.
3 Rub fat into flour until like breadcrumbs.
4 Add sugar. Mix.
5 Mix to a very stiff dough with beaten egg (it may not be necessary to add all the egg, depending on its size).
6 Roll the dough into a long sausage shape on a floured board.
7 Divide into 8–10 sections, roll each section into a ball. Place on a greased baking sheet.
8 Make a deep impression with the finger or wooden spoon handle in the centre of each bun.
9 Fill each hole with jam (about a teaspoonful).
10 Bake for 15–20 mins. Test as for rock buns. Cool on a wire tray.
11 Serve on a plate with a doyley.

CHOCOLATE BUNS

100 g S.R. flour   *25 g cocoa*
50 g margarine   *½ beaten egg*
50 g sugar

1 Oven 400°F/Gas Mark 6. Prepare a baking sheet or 10 bun tins.
2 Sieve flour and cocoa into a mixing bowl.
3 Rub margarine into flour until like breadcrumbs.
4 Add sugar and mix.
5 Mix to a stiff dough with beaten egg.
6 Either pile into bun tins or on a baking tray.
7 Bake 15–20 mins. Test as for rock buns. Cool on a wire tray.
8 Serve on a plate with a doyley.

FARMHOUSE FRUIT CAKE

250 g S.R. flour   *125–175 g mixed fruit*
½ teasp. mixed spice   *2 eggs*
125 g margarine   *2 tablesp. milk*
125 g sugar

1 Oven 350°F/Gas Mark 4. Grease and line a 15 cm loaf tin.
2 Sieve flour and spice into a mixing bowl.
3 Rub fat into flour and spice.

4 Add sugar and fruit.
5 Mix to a dropping consistency with the beaten egg and milk.
6 Place into the loaf tin.
7 Bake for 1 hr. to 1¼ hrs. Test by piercing a warmed skewer into the centre of the cake. If the skewer is left clean, the cake is cooked. Also note colour of cake and any signs of it shrinking from the sides.
8 Remove from tin and cool on a wire tray.
9 Serve sliced on a plate with a doyley.
  The slices can be spread with butter.

N.B. A cherry or coconut cake can be made in the same way by substituting glacé cherries or coconut for the fruit.

SCONES

½ *level teasp. salt*
1 *level teasp. baking powder*
250 *g S.R. flour*
25–50 *g margarine*
25–50 *g sugar*
125 *ml milk*
1 *egg (optional)*

Plain flour may be used with the addition of 3 level teasp. baking powder or 2 teasp. cream of tartar, and 1 teasp. bicarb. of soda; or 1 teasp. cream of tartar, 1 teasp. bicarb. of soda and sour milk

1 Oven 450°F/Gas Mark 8. Grease a baking sheet.
2 Sieve salt, baking powder and flour into a mixing bowl.
3 Rub fat into flour until like breadcrumbs.
4 Add sugar. Mix.
5 Mix to a dough with milk and beaten egg if used, leaving a little for glazing. Knead until dough is smooth.
6 Roll out on a floured board to 1 cm in thickness. Cut with a 5 cm fluted cutter.
7 Place on the baking sheet. Brush with egg or milk.
8 Bake 7–10 mins. Test by knocking the bottom of the scone; a hollow sound indicates that the scone is ready.
9 Serve halved and buttered on a plate with a doyley.

Variations

FRUIT OR CHERRY SCONES

50 g currants or chopped glacé cherries may be added with the sugar.

CHEESE SCONES

The sugar is omitted and 50 g of finely grated cheese is added when the mixture has reached the breadcrumb stage. A ¼ teasp. dry mustard may also be added. A plain 5 cm cutter is used for this type of savoury scone. Serve buttered on a dish paper garnished with parsley.

GIRDLE SCONES

Follow basic scone recipe but roll dough out a little thinner in order to make 12–16 scones cut in triangles.

1 Clean a girdle pan or hot plate or frying pan by scouring with salt and dusting clean with soft paper.
2 Heat girdle or frying pan to moderate heat; put hot plate on low.
3 Dust triangular shapes with flour.
4 Test heat by holding the hand 1 cm above pan or hot plate. If your hand feels a comfortable warmth, the heat is right.
5 Place scones on the hot plate one at a time. Cook for 7–8 mins. on each side.
6 The scones appear golden brown on each side and springy when pinched.
7 Serve hot in a folded table napkin. Serve butter pats in a separate dish.

DROPPED SCONES

250 g S.R. flour
1 level teasp. baking powder
50 g caster sugar or golden syrup.

50 g margarine
1 egg
Approx. 250 ml milk

1 Prepare and pre-heat girdle pan, hot plate or frying pan as for girdle scones.
2 Prepare a small knob of lard for greasing the girdle.
3 Sieve flour and baking powder into a mixing bowl.
4 Rub fat into flour until like breadcrumbs. Add sugar if used.
5 Add egg, 180 ml of the milk and syrup, if used. Mix all to a batter.
6 The batter should just settle to its own level. Add remaining milk if necessary.

7 Test girdle pan. Grease; the grease should give a blue haze.
8 Pour neat circles with a tablespoon over the girdle pan. When the batter bubbles and rises, breaking the surface, the scones must be turned over with a palette knife.
9 Both sides should be golden.
10 Keep hot in a tea towel.
11 Serve hot with butter.

AMERICAN DOUGHNUTS

250 g S.R. flour   *1 egg*
50 g margarine   *2 tablesp. milk*
50 g sugar   *Caster sugar and cinnamon*

1 Prepare a deep fat frying basket.
2 Sieve flour into a mixing bowl.
3 Rub fat into flour until like breadcrumbs.
4 Add sugar, mix.
5 Mix to a dry soft dough with beaten egg and milk. Knead.
6 Roll out to 1 cm thick on a floured board.
7 Cut into circles with a 5 cm plain cutter. Cut another small hole from the centre, 1.5 cm in diameter.
8 Heat fat until it browns bread in 20 secs. Fry doughnuts for 10 mins. until well risen firm and golden brown.
9 Drain well and toss in caster sugar with a little powdered cinnamon.
10 Serve hot as they are or cold piped with fresh cream in the centre.

SHWETSCHEN KUCHEN

250 g S.R. flour   *25 g melted butter*
1 level teasp. baking powder   *or margarine*
100 g caster sugar   *1 kilo stoned plums or 750 g*
100 g butter or margarine   *sliced apples or a large tin of*
1 large egg   *fruit, drained*
125 ml milk   *Granulated sugar*

N.B. This recipe makes 1 large or 2 small cakes.

1 Oven 400°F/Gas Mark 6. Grease two 14 cm loose-bottomed sandwich tins or a rectangular tin 18 cm x 30 cm.

2 Sieve dry ingredients into a mixing bowl. Rub in the butter. Add the sugar.
3 Beat the egg, stir in the milk and then add to the dry ingredients. Mix to a smooth dough.
4 Spread into the tin. Brush the surface with the melted butter. Stone and halve the plums or core and slice apples and arrange over the surface of the mixture. Sprinkle with granulated sugar.
5 Cook the larger cake for 40 mins., the smaller for 30 mins. until the cake has risen, is golden brown, a skewer comes out clean and pudding has shrunk from the sides of the tin.
6 Sugar well. Serve hot as a pudding or cold as a cake with whipped cream.

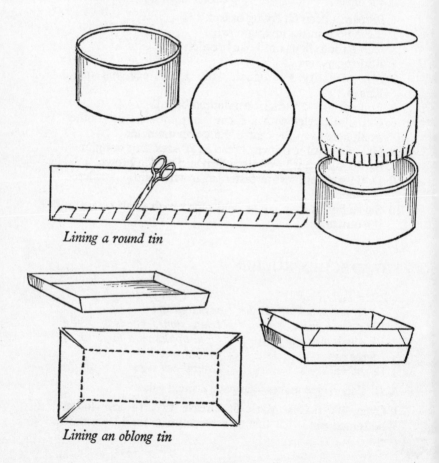

Lining a round tin

Lining an oblong tin

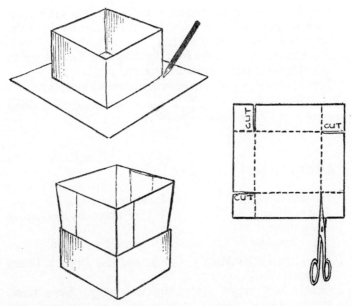

Lining a square tin

Cakes made by the melting method

GINGERBREAD

25 g margarine	1½ teasp. ground ginger
50 g brown sugar (Barbados or Demerara)	1 level teasp. bicarbonate of soda
150 g syrup	1 egg
200 g plain flour	Approx. 4–5 tablesp. milk

1 Oven 350°F/Gas Mark 4. Grease and line a 16 cm square Gingerbread tin.
2 Gently warm fat, sugar and syrup in a pan until the fat has just melted. Do not boil or the gingerbread will be hard.
3 Sieve flour, ginger and bicarbonate of soda into a mixing bowl. Make a well in the centre.
4 Pour cooled syrup mixture into the bowl. Mix well.
5 Add beaten egg and half of the milk. Mix to a smooth batter to coat the back of a wooden spoon. Add more milk if necessary.

6 Pour mixture into the tin. Bake $\frac{3}{4}$ hr.–1 hr. The cake when cooked feels firm to the touch and has shrunk from the sides of the tin. Cool in the tin.
7 Store in an air-tight tin for a few days for the texture to become moist and spongy and the crust soft.
8 Serve cut into square pieces on a plate with a doyley.

N.B. Fruit gingerbread may be made by adding 50 g dried fruit with the syrup mixture.

PARKIN

75 g brown sugar
75 g margarine
150 g syrup
50 g plain flour

1 level teasp. ginger
1 level teasp. bicarbonate of soda
150 g medium oatmeal

1 Oven 350°F/Gas Mark 4. Grease and line 20 cm x 12 cm Yorkshire pudding tin.
2 Gently heat sugar, margarine and syrup. Sieve flour, ginger and bicarbonate of soda into a mixing bowl, add oatmeal, mix well. Make a well in the centre.
3 Add syrup mixture. Mix to a smooth batter.
4 Pour into prepared tin. Bake for $\frac{3}{4}$ hr.–1 hr. Test and cool as for gingerbread.
5 Store for a few days. Serve cut in square pieces on a plate with a doyley.

FLAPJACK

125 g rolled oats
75 g brown sugar

75 g margarine
2 tablesp. golden syrup

1 Oven 325°F/Gas Mark 3. Grease a 18 cm square shallow tin.
2 Melt fat, sugar and syrup. Add rolled oats in the pan. Mix well.
3 Press firmly into the tin. Bake 15–20 mins. until golden and set.
4 Whilst still warm, divide into fingers 2 cm x 6 cm. Cool in the tin.
5 When cool, remove from tin. Serve on a plate with a doyley.

Cakes made by the whisking method

Fatless sponges

SWISS ROLL

50 g caster sugar   *4 tablesp. jam*
2 eggs   *Caster sugar for dredging*
50 g S.R. or plain flour

1 Oven 400°F/Gas Mark 6. Line and grease a Swiss roll tin 18 cm x 30 cm.
2 Whisk sugar and eggs until thick and creamy (this may be done more quickly over a pan of hot water).
3 Sieve flour into the mixture. Fold in lightly with a metal spoon.
4 Pour into prepared tin. Place jam to warm.
5 Bake $\frac{2}{3}$ way up the oven for 7–10 mins. The sponge appears shrunken from the sides of the tin and bounces back into position when lightly pressed.
6 Turn out on to a sugared greaseproof paper.
7 Trim off the edges. Spread with warmed jam.
8 Fold over the short end and pull over the greaseproof paper and roll away from you.
9 Dredge with caster sugar. Cool.
10 Serve on a plate with a doyley.

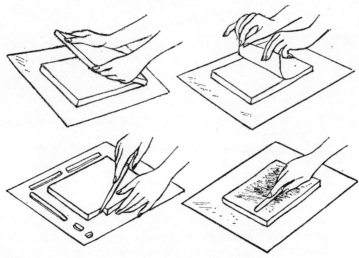

Swiss roll—turning out, trimming and spreading

Finishing a Swiss roll

Variation

CHOCOLATE SWISS ROLL

Substitute 15 g cocoa for 15 g flour. Fill with butter cream.
See Yule Log.

SPONGE FRUIT FLAN

2 eggs
50 g caster sugar
50 g S.R. or plain flour

1 tin fruit or fresh fruit plus
125 ml syrup made from sugar
and water (see Fruit Salad)
1 rounded teasp. arrowroot
Glacé cherries for decoration

1 Oven 400°F/Gas Mark 6. Grease and line centre only of a
  20 cm sponge flan tin.
2 Whisk eggs and sugar. Fold in flour as for Swiss roll.
3 Pour into tin. Bake centre of the oven for 20 mins. Test
  by pressing lightly.
4 Turn out and cool on a wire tray.
5 Strain juice from tin of fruit or prepare syrup from sugar
  and water. Arrange fruit in flan case. Make up the fruit
  juice to 125 ml with water or pour excess juice to one side.
6 Blend a little of the juice or syrup with the arrowroot in a
  small pan. Gradually add remaining juice or syrup.

7 Heat gently, stirring all the time until liquid boils and thickens. Cook for 2 mins. until liquid becomes clear. Cool slightly.

8 Spoon glaze over the fruit. Decorate with a glacé cherry.

9 Serve on a plate with a doyley. The centre of the doyley must first be removed. Serve with fresh cream which may be piped on the outside rim of the flan.

SPONGE CAKE OR SANDWICH

3 eggs
75 g caster sugar
75 g S.R. or plain flour

2 tablesp. jam
Extra caster or icing sugar for dredging

1 Oven 400°F/Gas Mark 6. Grease and line two 15 cm sandwich tins.

2 Whisk eggs and sugar. Fold in the flour.

3 Divide mixture between two tins. Bake half way up the oven for 20 mins. Test by pressing lightly.

4 Turn out and cool on a wire tray.

5 Sandwich together with jam. Sprinkle with caster sugar or sieved icing sugar.

6 Serve on a plate with a doyley.

SPONGE DROPS OR FINGERS

2 eggs
50 g caster sugar
50 g S.R. flour

3 tablesp. jam and whipped cream for filling
Icing sugar for sprinkling

1 Oven 350°F/Gas Mark 4. Grease baking tins (sponge drops) or sponge finger tins.

2 Whisk eggs and sugar, fold in the flour.

3 Spoon mixture into finger tins or space dessertspoons of the mixture on the baking tray, 1 dessertspoonful per drop.

4 Bake middle shelf for 7–10 mins. Test by pressing lightly.

5 Cool on a wire tray. Sandwich two fingers or drops together with jam and/or cream. Sprinkle with sieved icing sugar.

6 Serve on a plate with a doyley.

N.B. The fingers or drops may be used in a trifle if cream is omitted.

YULE LOG

3 eggs	*75 g butter cream for filling*
75 g caster sugar	*150 g melted chocolate or 100 g*
50 g S.R. flour	*chocolate butter cream (see*
15 g cocoa	*icings) for spreading*

1 Oven 400°F/Gas Mark 6. Grease and line 24 cm x 33 cm Swiss roll tin.
2 Whisk eggs and sugar. Fold in sieved flour and cocoa.
3 Pour into prepared tin. Bake ⅔ way up the oven for 7–10 mins. Test as for Swiss roll.
4 Prepare a sheet of greaseproof paper slightly larger than the size of the tin and dredge in caster sugar.
5 Turn cake out on to the paper, trim edges. Roll up with the paper by folding over the edge nearest you (i.e. the shortest edge), and rolling firmly and in a straight line away from you. The paper must be rolled up with the cake. Leave to cool.
6 Prepare butter creams and melted chocolate if used.
7 When cool, unroll cake, remove paper. Spread with plain butter cream, re-roll.
8 Coat finished roll with chocolate butter cream or melted chocolate. Decorate with a fork to give a woody texture. Sprinkle sieved icing sugar on top to give the impression of snow. Finish off with a sprig of almond paste holly or silver balls.
9 Serve on a silver cake board.

Creaming method of cake making

Rich cakes

VICTORIA SANDWICH

100 g margarine	*baking powder*
100 g caster sugar	*Jam for filling*
2 eggs	*Icing sugar for dredging*
100 g S.R. flour or 100 g plain	
flour plus ¼ teasp. baking powder.	

1 Oven 375°F/Gas Mark 5. Grease and line two 15 cm sandwich tins.

2 Cream margarine and sugar with a wooden spoon until mixture is white and fluffy and drops off the spoon to the count of two.
3 Beat the eggs in a basin.
4 Gradually add and beat in the eggs to the creamed mixture with a wooden spoon.
5 Sieve the flour. Fold into the mixture with a metal spoon.
6 Divide the mixture between the two tins.
7 Bake on the middle shelf for 20–25 mins. The cake when ready will appear slightly shrunken from the sides and bounces back to shape when pressed.
8 Turn out on a wire cooling tray. Cool.
9 Sandwich both layers together with jam. Sprinkle either with caster sugar or sieved icing sugar.
10 Serve on a round plate with a doyley.

CHOCOLATE SANDWICH

15 g of the flour may be replaced by 15 g cocoa. The layers may be sandwiched together with 75 g butter cream (see icings).

SMALL CAKES OR QUEEN CAKES

50 g margarine   *1 egg*
50 g caster sugar   *A little milk if necessary*
75 g S.R. flour

1 Oven 375°F/Gas Mark 5. Prepare 10–12 baking paper cases placing them in a bun tin.
2 Cream fat and sugar, beat in the egg, fold in the flour as for Victoria Sandwich. If the mixture is very stiff, add a little milk. Stir in lightly.
3 Divide mixture into the cases, approximately two teaspoons in each case.
4 Bake on the middle shelf for 15–20 mins. The cakes when ready will bounce back into position when lightly pressed.
5 Cool on a wire tray.
6 Decorate or sprinkle with sieved icing sugar as required.
7 Serve on a round plate with a doyley.

Variations

CHOCOLATE CAKES

Substitute 15 g cocoa for 15 g flour. Decorate with melted chocolate or pipe with butter cream (see icings).

FRUIT CAKES

25 g of sultanas or currants may be added after the egg has been beaten in.

COCONUT CAKES

25 g desiccated coconut may be added with the flour.

BUTTERFLY CAKES

Slice off a circular section from the top of the cakes. Divide circle into two (wings). Pipe or spread butter cream on top of each cake. Place wings either side of cream. Decorate with a small piece of glacé cherry or jam. Sprinkle with sieved icing sugar.

MADEIRA CAKE

150 g margarine	*200 g plain flour*
150 g caster sugar	*1 teasp. baking powder*
3 eggs	*Grated zest 1 lemon*
2 tablesp. milk	*Citron peel*

1 Oven 350°F/Gas Mark 4. Grease and line a 15 cm square or 18 cm round tin.
2 Cream margarine and sugar, beat in the eggs and milk, fold in the flour and baking powder as for Victoria Sandwich, adding the grated zest with the flour.
3 Place in the tin. Place citron peel on top.
4 Bake on the middle shelf for half an hour at 350°F or 4 and then for 1½ hrs at 325° or 3. Test with a warmed skewer as for Farmhouse Fruit Cake.
5 Cool on a wire tray.
6 Serve on a round plate with a doyley, whole or in slices.

Variations

ALMOND

Substitute 75 g ground almonds for 75 g flour and add 1 teasp. almond essence with the egg.

CHERRY

Add 100 g quartered glacé cherries with the flour.

COFFEE AND WALNUT

Add 2 tablesp. coffee essence after the eggs. Add 50 g chopped walnuts with the flour.

DUNDEE

Add 25 g ground almonds, 100 g sultanas, 75 g raisins, 100 g currants, 50 g candied peel, grated zest of 1 lemon, 25 g blanched split almonds.

Add all the above, except for the split almonds, after the eggs. Place split almonds over the surface of the cake after it has been baked for 1½ hrs.

GINGER

Add 100 g chopped preserved ginger with the flour.

CHRISTMAS CAKE

150 g butter	*50 g chopped preserved ginger*
150 g brown sugar	*75 g chopped almonds*
3 eggs	*100 g quartered glacé*
150 g sultanas	*cherries*
150 g currants	*200 g plain flour*
150 g raisins	*½ teasp. baking powder*
50 g mixed peel	

1 Oven 325°F/Gas Mark 3. Grease and line 18 cm round or 16 cm square cake tin.
2 Cream butter and sugar, beat in the eggs as for Victoria Sandwich.

9--ACB * *

3 Clean fruit.
4 Add fruit. Mix. Fold in the flour and baking powder.
5 Place mixture into cake tin.
6 Bake at 325° or 3 for 1 hr., 300° or 2 for 1 hr. Test with a skewer.
7 Cool in the tin. Cover with almond paste and decorate with royal icing. See icings.

N.B. After cooking keep in an airtight tin or wrapped in foil until required for finishing.

Biscuits

Biscuits made by the rubbing-in method

PLAIN BISCUITS

100 g plain flour
50 g margarine
50 g sugar

½ beaten egg
Caster or icing sugar for sprinkling

1 Oven 350°F/Gas Mark 4. Grease a baking tray.
2 Sieve flour into a mixing bowl. Rub fat into flour until like breadcrumbs.
3 Add sugar, mix.
4 Mix to a very stiff dough with beaten egg. Knead until smooth.
5 Roll out thinly on a floured board. Cut into shapes. Prick.
6 Place on the baking tray. Bake 10–15 mins. Test for firmness.
7 Cool on a wire tray. Sprinkle with caster sugar or sieved icing sugar.
8 Serve on a plate with a doyley.

Variations

The following ingredients may be added to the above recipe. They should be added with the sugar.

Fruit biscuits
Coconut biscuits
Cherry biscuits
Chocolate biscuits

50 g currants
50 g desiccated coconut
50 g glacé cherries
15 g cocoa substituted for 15 g flour

WHEATMEAL BISCUITS

250 g wheatmeal flour	½ teasp. vanilla essence
150 g margarine	Caster sugar or melted
25 g sugar	chocolate for finishing
1 beaten egg	

1 Oven 350°F/Gas Mark 4. Grease a baking tray.
2 Sieve flour into mixing bowl. Rub fat into flour until like breadcrumbs.
3 Add sugar, mix. Mix together to a stiff dough with beaten egg and vanilla essence. Knead until smooth.
4 Roll out thinly on a floured board. Cut with a 4 cm plain cutter. Place on a baking tray.
5 Prick. Bake for 15–20 mins. Test for firmness.
6 Cool on a wire tray. Sprinkle with caster sugar, or coat one side with melted chocolate.
7 Serve on a plate with a doyley or a biscuit tray.

SHORTBREAD

100 g plain flour with	50 g caster sugar
50 g rice flour or cornflour	100 g butter
or 150 g plain flour	Caster sugar for dredging

1 Oven 325°F/Gas Mark 3. Grease a baking tray.
2 Sieve flour, rice flour and caster sugar into a mixing bowl.
3 Rub butter into the dry ingredients until a dough is formed. Knead lightly.
4 Shape dough into a circle or oblong 1 cm thick.
5 Circle—flute edges. Divide circle into 8–10 sections.
   Fingers—cut fingers approximately 3 cm x 8 cm.
6 Place on a baking tray. Prick. Bake 20–25 mins. for fingers, 40–45 mins. for circle until a pale golden brown. If shortbread is allowed to brown too much it will have a bitter flavour. Test for firmness.
7 Cool, but whilst still warm, dredge in caster sugar. Serve on a plate with a doyley.

Biscuits made by melting method

BRANDY SNAPS

50 g margarine	¼ teasp. ground ginger
50 g fine brown sugar	1 teasp. lemon juice

50 g golden syrup   *Whipped cream for filling*
50 g flour

1 Oven 325°F/Gas Mark 3. Grease several baking trays.
2 Melt fat, sugar and syrup. Sieve flour and ginger. Add
  syrup mixture to the flour, beat to a thin batter, beat in
  lemon juice.
3 Drop teaspoonsful of the mixture 8 cm apart on the
  baking trays.
4 Bake until slightly set and golden brown, 7–10 mins.
5 Meanwhile, grease handle of a wooden spoon.
6 Whilst still warm, lift off tray with a palette knife and roll
  over the oiled handle. Remove handle and continue. This
  must be done very quickly, otherwise the brandy snaps
  will cool and harden, making it impossible to roll them.
7 When cold the centre can be filled with cream, piped into
  each end.
8 Serve on a round plate with a doyley.
N.B. Brandy snaps can be stored in an air-tight tin and
filled when required.

FRUIT COOKIES

50 g margarine $\frac{1}{2}$ level teasp. bicarbonate of
25 g brown sugar   soda
75 g golden syrup $\frac{1}{8}$ teasp. mixed spice
100 g plain flour   1 level teasp. ginger
                                  50 g dried fruit

1 Oven 350°F/Gas Mark 4. Grease two baking trays.
2 Melt margarine, sugar and syrup. Sieve all dry ingredients
  together. Make a well in the centre. Add syrup mixture
  and fruit. Beat well.
3 Leave to cool so that mixture may be rolled as a dough.
4 Roll teaspoonsful of mixture into walnut size balls.
5 Space 6 cm apart on a baking tray.
6 Bake 20 mins. until golden and set. They will not be crisp
  until cool. Leave to settle on the tin. Cool on a wire tray.
7 Serve on a plate with a doyley.

OAT COOKIES

50 g margarine $\frac{1}{2}$ level teasp. bicarbonate of
50 g brown sugar   soda
1 tablesp. golden syrup   50 g rolled oats
50 g plain flour $\frac{1}{4}$ teasp. vanilla essence

Method is as for fruit cookies. Mix oats with flour. Add essence with syrup mixture.

GINGERNUTS

50 g margarine
25 g brown sugar
25 g golden syrup
100 g plain flour

½ level teasp. bicarbonate of soda
1 level teasp. ginger

1 Oven 325°F/Gas Mark 3. Grease baking trays.
2 Melt margarine, sugar and syrup. Sieve all dry ingredients together. Add syrup mixture to dry ingredients. Beat well.
3 Place teaspoonsful of mixture 6 cm apart on baking trays. Bake 15–20 mins. until firm and golden.
4 Cool on a wire tray.
5 Serve on a round plate with a doyley.

N.B. To give a crinkled surface, remove from the oven 5 mins. before cooking completed and bang the tray once on a hard surface. Return to the oven.

Biscuits made by the creaming method

SHREWSBURY BISCUITS

100 g margarine
100 g caster sugar
1 egg

200 g S.R. flour
Grated zest 1 lemon
Caster sugar for dredging

1 Oven 350°F/Gas Mark 4. Grease a baking tray.
2 Cream margarine and sugar, beat in the egg. Fold in flour and lemon zest as for Victoria Sandwich.
3 Knead until smooth. Roll out thinly on a floured board.
4 Cut with a 4 cm fluted cutter. Place on a baking tray. Prick.
5 Bake 15–20 mins. until firm and golden. Cool on a wire tray.
6 Dredge with caster sugar whilst still warm.
7 Serve on a plate with a doyley.

Variations

EASTER BISCUITS

Add 1 teasp. cinnamon and 50 g currants after the egg.

ORANGE CREAMS

Substitute orange zest for the lemon zest. Sandwich two biscuits together with orange butter cream (see icings). Dredge with icing sugar.

COFFEE CREAMS

Substitute 1 teasp. coffee essence for lemon rind. Sandwich biscuits with coffee butter cream (see icings). Dredge with icing sugar.

CHOCOLATE CHIP COOKIES

75 g margarine
75 g brown sugar
1 egg
½ teasp. vanilla essence

150 g S.R. flour
½ teasp. salt
100 g plain chocolate chips

1 Oven 350°F/Gas Mark 4. Grease a baking tray.
2 Cream margarine and sugar. Beat in egg and essence. Fold in the sieved flour and salt.
3 Gently fold in chocolate chips.
4 Place apart in teaspoonsful on a baking tray. Bake 10–15 mins. until firm.
5 Cool on a wire tray. Serve on a plate with a doyley.

VIENNESE FINGERS

50 g margarine
50 g caster sugar

½ teasp. vanilla essence
150 g S.R. flour

Filling:
Jam or butter cream
Melted chocolate for dipping
ends

1 Oven 350°F/Gas Mark 4. Grease a baking tray.
2 Cream fat and sugar. Beat in essence. Fold in the flour.
3 Place mixture in a piping bag with a 1 cm star nozzle. Pipe fingers 8 cm long on to the baking tray.
4 Bake 20–25 mins. Cool on a wire tray.
5 Sandwich together with jam or butter cream. Dip ends in melted chocolate (see icings).
Serve on a round plate with a doyley.

N.B. **VIENNESE ROSETTES**—pipe rosettes, decorate with a glacé cherry.

MELTING MOMENTS

50 g margarine	*75 g S.R. flour*
50 g caster sugar	*Desiccated coconut for rolling*
1 egg	*Glacé cherries*
½ teasp. vanilla essence	

1 Oven 350°F/Gas Mark 4. Grease a baking tray.
2 Cream fat and sugar. Beat in egg and essence. Fold in the flour. Knead.
3 Roll mixture into a sausage shape. Divide into 20 pieces. Roll each piece into a ball, toss in coconut.
4 Place on a baking tray, press lightly to flatten. Decorate with ½ glacé cherry.
5 Bake 15–20 mins. Cool on a wire tray.
6 Serve on a plate with a doyley.

ALMOND RINGS

50 g margarine	*1 egg yolk*
25 g caster sugar	*100 g plain flour*
Topping:	
1 egg white	*75 g ground almonds*
75 g caster sugar	*Red jam*

1 Oven 350°F/Gas Mark 4. Grease a baking tray.
2 Cream fat and sugar, beat in egg yolk. Fold in flour. Knead until smooth.
3 Roll out thinly on a floured board. Cut with a 6 cm plain cutter.
4 Place on a baking tray. Prick.
5 Whisk egg white until frothy. Stir in sugar and almonds.
6 Place in a piping bag with a 1 cm star pipe. Pipe a circle around the top of each biscuit.
7 Bake 15–20 mins. until firm. Cool on a wire tray.
8 Finish off with a little red jam in the middle of each biscuit.
9 Serve on a plate with a doyley.

BOURBON BISCUITS

50 g margarine	*15 g cocoa*
50 g caster sugar	*1 tablesp. honey*

½ *level teasp. bicarbonate of*   *100 g plain flour*
soda   *Icing sugar for dredging*

Filling:
90 g icing sugar   *50 g margarine*
10 g cocoa   *1 teasp. coffee essence*

1 Oven 325°F/Gas Mark 3. Grease a baking tray.
2 Cream margarine and sugar. Beat in the honey. Sieve flour, cocoa and bi-carbonate of soda. Fold into the mixture to form a stiff paste.
3 Knead well. Roll out thinly on a floured board to an oblong shape.
4 Cut into fingers 10 cm x 4 cm. Place on baking tray. Prick. Bake 15–20 mins. until firm. Cool on a wire tray.
5 Sieve icing sugar and cocoa, cream with margarine and coffee essence for filling.
6 Sandwich cooled biscuits together with the filling.
7 Dredge with icing sugar.
8 Serve on a plate with a doyley.

Icings

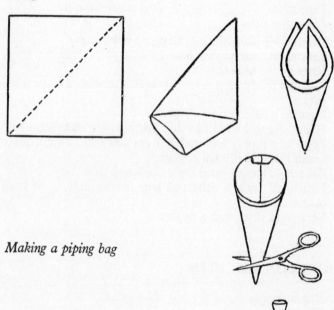

Making a piping bag

Use of various tubes

Suggestions for piping designs

GLACÉ ICING

150 g icing sugar	*Colouring*
5–6 teasp. warm water or	
fruit juice	

1 Sieve icing sugar into a large basin.
2 Gradually add water, one teaspoonful at a time, until

mixture will coat the back of a wooden spoon. Add colouring with a skewer after the first teaspoonful of water to ensure that the icing will not be too thin.

3 Use to ice Victoria Sandwiches and small buns.

ROYAL ICING

500 g icing sugar
2–3 egg whites

Soft icing to be kept
Add 2 teasp. glycerine, 2 teasp. lemon juice.

Hard icing for piping
Add 2 drops acetic acid.

For coating a cake the icing using glycerine is recommended.

For piping acetic acid may be added but can be omitted.

Lemon juice gives a pleasant flavour but gives a hard brittle icing when kept.

1 Sieve icing sugar into a mixing bowl.
2 Whisk 2 eggs whites slightly in a clean bowl free of any grease.
3 Work half the sugar into the egg whites. Beat vigorously until it loses the yellow tinge of the egg whites.
4 Gradually work in the rest of the sugar and if necessary the third egg white—until icing coats the back of the spoon and reaches its own level slowly.
5 Cover the icing at once with a damp cloth. Leave to stand for 10 mins. to allow bubbles to escape. This consistency of icing when put on a cake will find its own level when shaken.

For piping the icing should be beaten until it stands in peaks.

ALMOND PASTE

125 g caster sugar
125 g icing sugar
250 g ground almonds
1 egg

1 tablesp. lemon juice
¼ teasp. vanilla essence
⅛ teasp. almond essence

1 Sieve sugars and almonds into a mixing bowl to remove any brown flakes from the almonds. Mix well together.
2 Beat the egg. Add essences and flavourings to the dry ingredients.

3 Gradually stir in the egg to form a soft paste. The almond paste becomes stiff after a short while. It must be neither sticky nor so dry that it cracks at the edges.
4 Knead paste until quite smooth.
5 Store in a plastic bag to prevent it from drying.
6 Use as a covering for Christmas cakes, Battenberg cakes or Almond Paste sweets. Colouring may be added with the essences if desired.

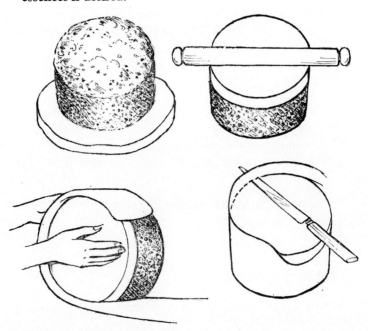

Putting almond paste on a cake

APRICOT GLAZE

250 g apricot jam
1 tablesp. lemon juice

1–2 tablesp. water (depending on consistency of jam)

1 Warm jam gently in a pan. Pass through a wire sieve.
2 Return to the pan, add lemon juice and 1 tablesp. water. Bring it just to boiling point.
3 Add more boiling water if glaze is too thick (glaze should be sticky while still hot).
4 Use whilst still hot to prepare cakes for icing or as a glaze for fruit, etc.

AMERICAN FROSTING

250 g granulated sugar   *2 tablesp. water*
1 egg white   *1 tablesp. fruit juice*

1 Place all ingredients in a mixing bowl.
2 Place mixing bowl over a pan of hot water and whisk ingredients together until mixture stands in stiff peaks. About 7 mins. whisking time.
3 Colouring may be added if desired.
4 Use to cover cakes, e.g. Chocolate Victoria Sandwich. Rough up all over with a fork.

BUTTER CREAM

75 g icing sugar   *50 g butter*
$\frac{1}{2}$ *teasp. vanilla essence*

1 Sieve icing sugar into a mixing bowl.
2 Add butter. Cream together with a wooden spoon until the mixture is soft and creamy in texture and white in colour. Add essence.
3 Use as a filling and decoration for cakes.

Variations

ORANGE CREAM

Add orange colouring and the zest and juice of $\frac{1}{2}$ orange to the completed icing.

LEMON CREAM

Add lemon colouring, zest and juice of $\frac{1}{2}$ lemon to the completed icing. The consistency may need to be corrected by adding more icing sugar.

COFFEE CREAM

Add 2 level teasp. instant coffee powder or 1 teasp. coffee essence.
Sieve powder with the icing sugar or add essence to the finished cream.

CHOCOLATE CREAM

Add 2 level teasp. cocoa or chocolate powder. Sieve powder with icing sugar.

Use of a skewer in adding colourings
Plunge a clean skewer into the colouring. Add to icings or butter cream in the same way.

WHIPPED CREAM

125 ml double cream   *2 drops vanilla essence*
1 teasp. caster sugar   *(optional)*
(optional)

1 Place all ingredients in a mixing bowl.
2 Whip cream lightly until it will stand in smooth peaks. Whipping must then stop at once. Over-whipping causes the cream to separate out. The time of whipping depends upon the age of the cream. Fresh cream whips very quickly.
3 Whip just before use or store cream in a cool place until used.

Uses—pipe on to trifles, flans, cakes, etc. Use as a filling for cakes.

EXTENDED WHIPPED CREAM

1 egg white   *1 level teasp. caster sugar*
125 ml double cream   *½ teasp. vanilla essence*

1 Place all ingredients in a clean, dry mixing bowl.
2 Whip up until a stiff cream double in bulk is produced.
3 Use as for whipped cream.

MOCK CREAM

25 g custard powder or   *50 g butter*
cornflour   *50 g caster sugar*
125 ml milk   *Vanilla essence*

1 Blend custard powder or cornflour with a little of the milk in a small pan.

2 Gradually add all the milk. Heat until it boils and thickens, stirring all the time. Cook for 2 mins.
3 Place custard into a basin. Cover surface with damp greaseproof paper (see sauces).
4 Cream fat and sugar until white and fluffy. Add essence.
5 Whisk cooled custard until it is soft and creamy.
6 Gradually beat the custard into the butter cream, 1 teaspoonful at a time until all the custard is beaten in.
7 Use the same day. Use as for whipped cream.

CONFECTIONER'S CUSTARD

1 egg yolk   *2 drops vanilla essence*
15 g sugar   *greaseproof paper*
25 g flour   *few chopped nuts or glacé*
125 ml milk   *cherries*

1 Whisk egg and sugar until fairly thick.
2 Whisk in flour.
3 Heat the milk, whisk into the egg mixture. Return to pan, boil well whisking until thick.
4 Add essence. Cover surface with damp greaseproof paper.
5 Chopped nuts or glacé cherries may be added.
6 Use as a filling for tarts, custard slices, etc.

MELTED CHOCOLATE

150 g milk or plain chocolate

This quantity is sufficient to coat the surface of a 18 cm round or 15 cm square cake.

1 Grate chocolate on the coarse side of the grater. Place chocolate chips in a basin.
2 Select a pan into which the bottom half of the basin will fit tightly.
3 Half fill the pan with water. Place basin in the pan.
4 Gently heat the water to simmering point.
5 Turn heat off. Keep chocolate over the water until melted.
6 Do not over-heat. Do not let any water come in contact with the chocolate.
7 Use whilst still warm to coat cakes, biscuits, éclairs, etc.

14

Yeast mixtures

Points to consider when choosing yeast

1 Always try to buy fresh baker's yeast. The freshness can
be tested in the following ways:
   (a) Smell—this should be fairly strong and similar to
   alcohol.
   (b) Colour—fresh yeast is a pale fawny colour.
   (c) Texture—fresh yeast crumbles easily in the fingers.
2 Dried yeast can be used. Follow instructions on the
packet.

Proportions of yeast to use

15 g yeast to 250–500 g flour
25 g yeast to 1½ kilo flour (1,500 g)

PLAIN WHITE BREAD

500 g strong plain flour   *250 ml water*
2 level teasp. salt   *15 g yeast*

1 Warm and grease two 500 g loaf tins.
2 Warm flour. Sieve flour and salt into mixing bowl.
3 Boil 80 ml of the water. Add to remaining cold water.
This ensures that the water is at blood heat.
4 Mix yeast with 1 teasp. of the tepid water. Add remaining water to it, making sure the yeast is mixed in well.
5 Make a well in centre of the flour.
6 Pour yeast and water mixture into the well.
7 Draw the flour from the sides of the bowl into the well
with the hands.

8 Beat the flour into the yeast with the hands until an elastic dough is formed and the hands are free of any dough. Add more water if necessary.

9 Turn out on to a floured board. Knead well by lifting one end of the dough and rubbing it heavily over the other end with the palm of the hand. Repeat the process vigorously for 5 mins. The dough will appear smooth and very elastic when kneaded sufficiently well.

10 Place dough back in the mixing bowl. Cover with damp muslin or tea towel. Put to rise in a warm place for 40–45 mins. until dough has doubled in size. Suitable places for rising are (a) airing cupboard, (b) drying cabinet (c) over a bowl of hot water, (d) warming drawer of a cooker, (e) on the hearth, (f) cool rising in the refrigerator overnight. The temperature for rising must not exceed 90°F/32°C.

11 Oven, Gas Mark 8 or 450°F.

12 Remove dough from the warm place. Re-knead as before for 5 mins.

13 Divide into two. Shape into loaves and place in the greased tins.

14 Place tins in the warm place once more to prove for 15–20 mins. until they have doubled in size.

15 Either dust the loaves with flour (soft crust) or brush with cold water (hard crust). If a crisp crust is desired, leave bread as it is.

16 Bake bread in the upper half of the oven for 35–40 mins. until it has a golden brown crust. Test by knocking the bottom—hollow sound indicates that the bread is cooked.

17 Cool on a wire tray.

N.B. Bread may be risen inside a well-oiled plastic bag.

Cottage loaf

QUICKLY MADE BREAD

Follow the recipe and method for Plain White Bread, but vary as follows after instruction 9:

1 Shape bread and place in tins after the first kneading. Place to rise for 40–45 mins. until it has doubled in size.
2 Finish off the crust. Bake as above—thus omitting the proving stage.
3 The long method gives a better textured bread.

WHOLEMEAL BREAD

500 g wholemeal flour or *15 g brown sugar*
250 g white flour and 250 g *15 g margarine*
wholemeal flour *250 ml water*
2 teasp. salt *15 g yeast*

Method is as for white bread. Mix sugar in with the flour. Rub margarine into the flour before making the well in the centre.

BREAD ROLLS (HARD)

Use ½ basic recipe (with 15 g yeast).

1 Oven Gas Mark 8 or 450°F. Grease two baking trays.
2 Prepare dough as for white bread until rising stage completed. Knead for 2 mins.
3 Divide dough into 8 pieces. Shape into rounds, sausage shapes, knots, catherine wheels, scrolls, twists or plaits (see diagrams).
4 Prove 15–20 mins. until dough has doubled in size.
5 Brush over with cold water.
6 Bake for 15–20 mins. until rolls are golden brown and give a hollow sound when knocked.
7 Cool on a wire tray.
8 Serve in a bread basket lined with a table napkin.

Rolling into a ball
10—ACB * *

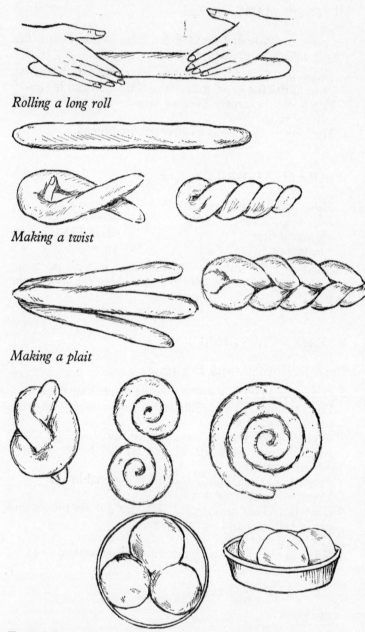

Rolling a long roll

Making a twist

Making a plait

From left to right: *single knot, letters, Catherine wheel, Shamrock loaf*

MILK BREAD

500 g strong plain flour   *15 g yeast*
2 level teasp. salt   *Beaten egg for glazing or*
15 g lard   *margarine for brushing*
250 ml milk

1 Grease tins or baking trays.
2 Warm flour. Sieve flour and salt into a mixing bowl.
3 Rub lard into the flour. Make a well in the centre.
4 Boil 80 ml of the milk. Add remaining milk.
5 Mix yeast with the warm liquid.
6 Pour yeast liquid into the well. Mix dough as for white bread.
7 Knead for 5 mins. Cover with a damp cloth. Place to rise for 40–45 mins. until it has doubled in size.
8 Oven Gas Mark 8 or 450°F.
9 Turn dough out onto a floured board. Re-knead for 5 mins. Shape into loaves or rolls. Place in loaf tins or on baking trays.
10 Place in a warm place to prove for 15–20 mins.
11 Brush over with beaten egg if a brown shiny glaze is required. If a short but not shiny crust is required, brush over with melted margarine after baking.
12 Bake for 20 mins. for rolls, 35–40 mins. for loaves. Test as for white bread.
13 Cool on a wire tray.
14 Serve as for bread rolls or loaves.

Variations

DINNER ROLLS

Divide dough into 16 pieces. Shape into fancy rolls (see diagrams). Brush over with beaten egg. Bake as for bread rolls.

BRIDGE ROLLS

Roll dough into an oblong 1.5 cm thick. Cut the dough into 6 cm. length strips. Divide each strip into fingers 1.5 cm wide. Roll each finger a little, tapering at the ends. Place closely together on a baking tray, so that they will join up when risen. Bake as for bread rolls. Do not separate until cool. Cool in a clean cloth to keep soft and moist.

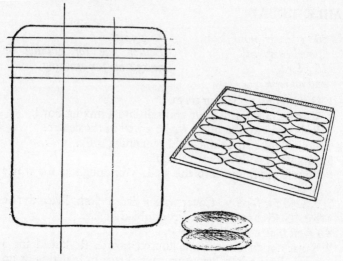

Bridge rolls

HUFFKINS

Divide the dough into 16 pieces. Shape into flat oval shapes. Dredge in flour. Make a hole in the centre with one finger. Rise and bake as for bread rolls. Cool in a clean cloth.

SCOTS BAPS

Divide the dough into 16 pieces. Shape into flat round shapes. Dredge in flour. Make two holes in the centre. Rise and bake as for bread rolls. Cool in a clean cloth.

Top left, *Bloomer;* right, *Coburg*
Bottom, left to right: *Boatshape, Bap, Huffkin*

CURRANT BREAD

Add 25 g sugar and 50 g currants after rubbing in the fat. Shape bread into two loaves. Bake in 500 g loaf tins. Brush over with beaten egg. Bake as for white bread.

CORNISH SPLITS

Divide dough into 18 pieces. Shape into balls. Set them close together, flatten slightly. Bake and cool as for Bridge Rolls. Brush with melted fat after baking, whilst still hot.

Yeast Bun Dough

PLAIN TEACAKES

250 g strong plain flour　　*25 g margarine*
½ level teasp. salt　　　　*15 g yeast*
½ level teasp. mixed spice　*6 tablesp. milk*
25 g sugar　　　　　　　　*1 egg*

1 Grease a baking tray.
2 Warm flour. Sieve flour, salt and spice into a mixing bowl.
3 Add sugar. Mix into the flour. Rub in the margarine. Make a well in the centre.
4 Cream yeast with a little of the milk. Add to remaining milk—keeping 1 tablesp. of the milk back.
5 Beat egg. Add to the milk. Pour liquid into the well. Mix dough as for white bread, adding the extra tablesp. of milk if necessary. Knead for 5 mins.
6 Place to rise in a warm place, covered with a damp cloth, for 40–45 mins.
7 Oven, Gas Mark 7 or 425°F.
8 Turn out on a floured board, re-knead for 5 mins.
9 Shape into 4 flat round cakes. Place on baking trays.
10 Put in a warm place to prove, 20 mins.
11 Bake 20–25 mins. Test for hollow sound.
12 Cool on a wire tray. Serve with butter.

Variations

FRUIT TEA CAKES

Add 50 g currants, 25 g mixed chopped peel, after rubbing in the fat.

CURRANT BUNS

Add 50 g currants after rubbing in the fat. Divide dough into 8. Shape into balls. Bake as for tea cakes. Brush over with sugar dissolved in milk after baking, whilst still hot.

HOT CROSS BUNS

250 g plain tea cake dough   *25 g short crust pastry*
25 g sugar   *Sugar and milk for glazing*
75 g currants } *for filling*
25 g margarine }

1 Grease a baking tray.
2 Prepare tea cake dough. Place to rise, 40–45 mins.
3 Oven Gas Mark 7 or 425°F.
4 Cream fat and sugar together, add currants.
5 Turn dough out onto a floured board.
6 Place creamed fat and sugar in the centre. Knead into the dough. Knead vigorously for 5 mins. until currants are evenly distributed.
7 Divide dough into 8. Shape into balls. Place on a baking tray. Brush with water.
8 Roll pastry out, cut into thin string-like strips. Decorate each bun with a cross of pastry strips.
9 Prove 15–20 mins. Bake for 20–25 mins. Test for a hollow sound.
10 Brush over with sugar dissolved in milk after baking, whilst still hot.
11 Cool on a wire tray. Serve with butter.

DOUGH CAKE

250 g tea cake dough, as   *50 g brown sugar*
p. 149, but using   *150 g mixed fruit*
25 g yeast   *Glacé icing*
50 g margarine

1 Grease an 18 cm round cake tin.
2 Prepare tea cake dough, using the extra yeast. Place to rise 40–45 mins.
3 Oven Gas Mark 7 or 425°F.
4 Cream fat and sugar, add fruit as for Hot Cross Buns.
5 Turn dough out on a floured board. Knead in fat and sugar and fruit, as for Hot Cross Buns.
6 Shape dough into a circular shape. Place in the cake tin. Prove for 20–30 mins.
7 Bake for 20–30 mins. until well browned at 425°F. or Regulo 7 then at 350°F. or Gas Mark 4 for 25–30 mins. Test for a hollow sound.
8 Cool on a wire tray.
9 Ice with glacé icing. (See icings.)
10 Serve on a plate with a doyley.

CHELSEA BUNS OR SWEDISH TEA RING

250 g strong plain flour   *½ egg*
½ level teasp. salt   *75 g margarine*
75 g caster sugar   *50 g currants*
15 g yeast   *½ teasp. mixed spice*
3 tablesp. milk   *Glacé icing*

1 Grease a roasting tin (Chelsea Buns) or baking tray (Swedish Tea Ring).
2 Prepare the bun dough as for tea cake, omitting the 25 g margarine and mixed spice but mixing dough with egg and milk. Knead dough for 5 mins. Place to rise 40–45 mins.
3 Cream remaining caster sugar and 50 g margarine together. And currants, peel and mixed spice.
4 Oven Gas Mark 7 or 425°F.
5 Turn dough out on to a floured board. Re-knead for 5 mins.
6 Roll dough out to a rectangle. Spread the remaining margarine over ⅔ of the dough. Fold as for flaky pastry (see pastries).
7 Roll dough out to 20 cm square. Spread the sugar, fat, currants and spice mixture over the square, leaving a 2 cm margin all around the edges.
8 Rolling away from you, roll the dough up tightly so that you end up with a thin sausage shape.

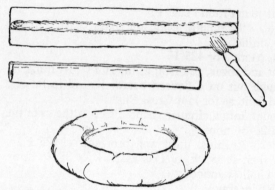

Swedish tea ring—shaping processes

CHELSEA BUNS

(a) Prepare a basin of warm water and a large French cook's knife.

(b) Dip the knife into the water and use it to divide the dough into 12 pieces.

(c) Set these fairly closely together with the cut edge facing upwards in a roasting tin.

(d) Prove for 20–25 mins. Bake 20–25 mins. Test for a hollow sound.

(e) Cool on a wire tray.

(f)   Ice before serving.

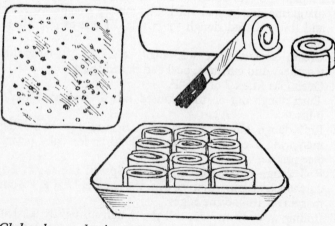

Chelsea buns—shaping processes

SWEDISH TEA RING

(a) Place the long sausage shape on a baking tray. Join the ends together forming a ring.

(b) Decorate the ring by cutting deeply into it with scissors at 2 cm intervals.

(c) Prove for 25–30 mins. Bake for 25–30 mins. Test for a hollow sound.

(d) Cool on a wire tray.

(e) Ice before serving.

Finishing Swedish tea ring and Chelsea buns

VARIATION OF SWEDISH TEA RING

Make a paste with 50 g ground almonds and 50 g sugar and hot water. Use in place of the currant and margarine mixture. Omit mixed spice. Serve iced and decorated with flaked almonds.

DOUGHNUTS

125 g strong plain flour
15 g caster sugar
10 g yeast
$\frac{1}{2}$ egg
2 tablesp. milk

2 tablesp. caster sugar
$\frac{1}{4}$ teasp. cinnamon

1 Prepare dough as for tea cakes till the rising stage is completed.

2 Knead for 5 mins. Rise for 1 hr.

3 Turn out on a floured board, re-knead for 5 mins.

4 Roll dough out to 1 cm thick. Cut into circles with a 5 cm plain cutter. Cut out a hole in the centre of each circle using a 1.5 cm cutter.

5 Place doughnuts on a greased baking sheet. Prove for 15–20 mins.

6 Prepare a deep fat frying pan. Heat fat until it browns bread in 20 secs. Sieve caster sugar and cinnamon on to piece of kitchen paper. Prepare a second clean sheet of kitchen paper with the sugar on a wire tray.

7 Place doughnuts carefully in the heated fat one at a time. Do not cook more than 3–5 doughnuts at a time, depending on the size of the pan.

8 Fry until golden brown and crisp, turning once during cooking.

9 Drain on clean kitchen paper. Toss in sugar. Cool on a wire tray.

10 Either serve as they are or fill centre with fresh cream. Serve on a plate, with a doyley.

15
Pastry

In recipes using pastry of any kind as part of the ingredients, the weight given to the pastry always refers to the amount of flour used in making up the pastry, e.g. 250 g short crust pastry means pastry made using 250 g flour and the other ingredients in proportion.

SHORT CRUST PASTRY

BASIC RECIPE

100 g plain flour
25 g margarine
25 g lard

4 teasp. cold water to mix
½ level teasp. salt

1 Oven 400°F/Gas Mark 6.
2 Sieve flour and salt together.
3 Add margarine and lard. Cut up into pieces using round bladed knife.
4 Rub fat into flour using finger tips.
5 Lift mixture above bowl to incorporate air.
6 As soon as mixture resembles fine breadcrumbs, stop rubbing in.
7 Add most of water, mixing with the round-bladed knife until pastry begins to stick together in a stiff dry dough.
8 Gather together, lightly, with finger tips and use as required.

Rolling out pastry

1 Make pastry into the approximate shape required; round ball if using on round plate, oblong if for an oblong dish or tin.
2 Lightly dredge the table or board and rolling pin with flour.
3 Roll the pastry with short, sharp strokes, keeping the shape required by moulding with the hands.

4 Always roll from front to back of table, turning the pastry, not the worker, to maintain an even shape and thickness of pastry.
5 Never dredge flour on to the pastry—always to the side and rub flour into the rolling pin well with the hand before beginning to roll.
6 Make sure the pastry does not stick to the table by continually moving it around. This is done when the direction of rolling is altered.
7 Never allow pastry to stick to the rolling pin. If this happens, scrape off the pastry using the back of a knife and re-flour the rolling pin.
8 Pastry should not be handled too much, otherwise it becomes tough and hard.
9 If pastry has to be left standing before use, cover with an up-turned mixing bowl or greaseproof paper.
10 Everything should be cold when making pastry and kept cool during the mixing.

Recipes using short crust pastry

JAM TARTLETS

100 g short crust pastry *¼ level teasp. salt*
4 teasp. cold water *3–4 tablesp. jam or lemon curd*

1 Oven 400°F/Gas Mark 6. Weigh ingredients.
2 Make short crust pastry.
3 Roll out ¼–½ cm thick, and, using a fluted cutter, cut out circles of pastry—larger than tins.
4 Line patty tins. There is no need to grease the tins.
5 Place approximately 1 teasp. jam or lemon curd in each tartlet.
6 Bake in pre-heated oven, top shelf for 10–15 mins. until pastry is pale golden in colour and firm to touch.
7 Cool on wire tray.
These tartlets may be served with whipped cream.

COCONUT TARTLETS

100 g short crust pastry *100 g caster sugar*
25 g apricot jam, sieved *50 g desiccated coconut*
2 egg whites
(1 whole egg)

1 Prepare oven 400°F/Gas Mark 6 and ingredients.
2 Make short crust pastry.
3 Roll out 1-½ cm thick and using a fluted cutter, cut out rounds—larger than tins.
4 Line patty tins.
5 Place about 1 teasp. jam in centre of each tart.
6 Put egg whites, sugar, coconut, into basin and beat for 5 mins.
7 Fill tartlets ¾ full with this mixture and using any pastry left over, put thin strips crossways on each tart.
8 Bake for 30 mins., reducing oven temperatures half way through if necessary, to 350°F/Gas Mark 4.
9 Tarts should be firm to touch and golden in colour.
10 Cool on wire tray.
Ground almonds and few drops almond essence may be used instead of coconut.

MINCE PIES

200 g short crust pastry   *1 egg white or water*
250 g mincemeat   *Caster sugar to glaze*

1 Oven 400°F/Gas Mark 6.
2 Make short crust pastry.
3 Roll out ¼-½ cm thick and cut out 12 rounds using a large cutter for the patty tins, and 12 smaller rounds to be used for lids.
4 Line the patty tins.
5 Place 1 teasp. mincemeat into each, but do not overfill.
6 Brush the undersides of the tops with beaten egg white or water; cover each pie and gently press edges together to seal.
7 Brush over with lightly beaten egg white or water; sprinkle with caster sugar.
8 Cut a hole in top of each pie with scissors or sharp knife.
9 Bake for 20–25 mins. until pale golden in colour and firm to touch. Mince pies may be eaten hot or cold. Instead of brushing with egg white or water and sprinkling caster sugar on top, they may be left and just lightly dredged with icing sugar when cold.
A mince tart, made on a plate using 100 g of pastry, makes a quick and useful sweet.

MANDARIN TARTLETS

100 g short crust pastry
1 tin mandarin oranges

1 teasp. arrowroot
To decorate—whipped cream if liked

1 Oven 400°F/Gas Mark 6.
2 Make short crust pastry.
3 Roll out ¼–½ cm thick, and cut out 12 rounds using fluted cutter.
4 Line patty tins carefully.
5 Prick over lightly with a fork and bake blind for 10–12 mins. until firm to touch.
6 Remove tartlets from tin and cool on wire tray.
7 Open tin of fruit. Drain carefully, reserving juice for glaze.
8 Arrange fruit neatly in pastry cases.
9 Blend arrowroot with little of juice. Bring rest of juice (using about 125 ml) to boil, pour over blended mixture and return to pan, stirring. Bring to boil and continue to cook and stir until mixture clears.
10 Spoon glaze over fruit in tartlets.
11 After cooling, whipped cream may be used to decorate. Other tinned fruit may be used instead of mandarin oranges; the method is the same. If fresh fruit is used, make a syrup of sugar and water as in sponge fruit flan.

MAIDS OF HONOUR

100 g short crust pastry
50 g butter or margarine
50 g sugar
50 g ground rice
1 egg

3 drops almond essence
Lemon curd
To decorate if liked—glacé icing and glacé cherries

1 Oven 375°F/Gas Mark 5.
2 Make pastry.
3 Roll out ¼–½ cm thick and using a fluted cutter, cut into rounds larger than the tins. Line patty tins.
4 Melt butter in saucepan. Add sugar, ground rice and egg, essence and mix well.
5 Place little lemon curd in each pastry case, then a teaspoonful of the mixture and bake for 20–30 mins. until firm.
6 Cool on a wire tray.
7 Decorate if liked with little glacé icing and a piece of glacé cherry.

COCONUT MERINGUE SLICES

250 g short crust pastry
100 g raspberry jam
2 egg whites

100 g caster sugar
100 g desiccated coconut

1 Oven 400°F/Gas Mark 6.
2 Make short crust pastry.
3 Roll out pastry to rectangular shape; line a Swiss Roll tin 18 cm x 30 cm. Trim edges. Prick all over with a fork.
4 Bake blind 10–12 mins.
5 Allow to cool. Spread jam on to pastry.
6 Reduce oven heat to 350°F/Gas Mark 4.
7 Make meringue, finally adding 75 g desiccated coconut.
8 Cover pastry with the meringue, using metal spoon or forcing bag fitted with star tube; sprinkle with rest of coconut.
9 Return to oven and cook until meringue is firm, and pale gold, about 25 mins.
10 Cool slightly and cut into fingers. Remove from tin and cool on wire tray.

OYSTERS

250 g short crust pastry
75 g margarine
75 g sugar
75 g ground almonds

$\frac{1}{4}$ teasp. almond essence
1 egg
Jam and cream
Icing sugar for dredging

1 Oven 350°F/Gas Mark 4.
2 Make short crust pastry.
3 Roll out pastry $\frac{1}{4}$–$\frac{1}{2}$ cm thick. Line patty tins. Cream margarine and sugar. Add ground almonds.
4 Add almond essence to egg.
5 Beat in a little at a time.
6 Place approximately 1 teaspoonful of mixture into each case.
7 Bake for 20 mins. until crisp.
8 Cool, and then remove filling from pastry case, using a sharp knife.
9 Place a little jam and pipe cream into the pastry and replace lid at an angle to resemble oysters.
10 Sprinkle with icing sugar.

HONEY NUT BOATS

250 g short crust pastry   1 teasp. coffee essence
75 g margarine   150 g coffee glacé icing
75 g caster sugar   Chopped nuts
1 tablesp. honey

1 Oven 400°F/Gas Mark 6. Prepare ingredients.
2 Make short crust pastry.
3 Place boat shaped patty tins on baking tray.
4 Put pastry over tins. Press into tins with finger. Use rolling pin to remove surplus pastry.
5 Prick bottoms and bake blind for 10–15 mins.
6 Meanwhile, cream margarine and sugar. Add almonds, honey and coffee essence.
7 Pipe into cooked pastry cases and leave in cool place until quite firm.
   Coat the top with coffee glacé icing and sprinkle chopped nuts down centre.

Variation on short crust pastry

CHEESE PASTRY

200 g plain flour   2–3 tablesp. water or egg yolk
1 level teasp. salt   (optional). The method is
Pinch cayenne pepper   exactly the same as for short
50 g lard   crust pastry. The grated
50 g margarine   cheese being added after the
or 100 g margarine only   fat has been rubbed in
50–100 g dry grated cheese

Recipes using cheese pastry

CHEESE STRAWS

100 g cheese pastry as above   Parsley for garnish
Cayenne pepper or paprika for
the ends (optional)

1 Oven 400°F/Gas Mark 6. Grease baking sheet.
2 Prepare pastry as for short crust, binding the ingredients together with beaten egg yolk.
3 Roll pastry to rectangle, $\frac{1}{4}$–$\frac{1}{2}$ cm thick.

4 Cut strips $\frac{1}{2}$ cm wide x 7–10 cm long.
5 Place the straws on the baking sheet in straight rows.
6 Using the scraps left over, roll again to $\frac{1}{4}$–$\frac{1}{2}$ cm thick and cut plain circles 4 cm across. Remove the centre of each circle with a 3 cm plain cutter and bake the remaining rings on the same tray as the straws.
7 Bake for 5–7 mins. until pale golden brown in colour and firm to touch.
8 Cool. To serve, place a bundle of straws through a ring and serve flat on a plate or standing up. OR the ends of the straws may be dipped in cayenne or paprika pepper and then built up to form a design.
Garnish either way with parsley.

CHEESE TWISTS

Made using same recipe as cheese straws.

1 Roll pastry to rectangle, but cut longer straws, 12 cm × 1.5 cm.
2 Each straw is then twisted holding them at each end.
3 Bake as above 5–7 mins.
4 Cool on a wire tray.

CHEESE BUTTERFLIES

200 g cheese pastry *Cayenne or paprika pepper*
50 g cream cheese *(optional)*
 Parsley for garnish

1 Oven 400°F/Gas Mark 6.
2 Make cheese pastry.
3 Using a 3–4 cm plain cutter, cut out biscuits and place on greased tray.
4 On half the biscuits only, cut across, but do not separate, the centre.
5 Bake for 5–7 mins. until pale golden brown and firm to touch. Separate halves.
6 Cool on a wire tray and sandwich two halves to a complete base, using cream cheese, so that the wings stand up.
7 Sprinkle little cayenne or paprika pepper in centre, using a skewer. Garnish with parsley.

11—ACB * *

Savoury Flans
Flans with a savoury filling may be made, using 100 g cheese
pastry. See lining a flan ring and baking blind.

RICH SHORT CRUST PASTRY OR FLAN
PASTRY

100 g plain flour	*25 g margarine or butter, 25 g*
½ level teasp. salt	*lard*
15 g caster sugar	*1 egg yolk*
	2 teasp. water, approximately

1 Make as for short crust pastry, the sugar being added to
  the flour before the fat is rubbed in.
2 Bind together using beaten egg yolk and a little extra
  water if necessary.
3 Roll out and use as required. Resting for 20 mins. before
  use helps rolling. It is more difficult to roll out owing to
  the presence of the egg yolk, and when baking this pastry
  the oven temperature should be reduced from 400°F/Gas
  Mark 6 after 15 mins. to 350°F/Gas Mark 4 because the
  presence of sugar makes it brown more quickly.

Lining a flan ring and baking blind
  1 Make 100 g rich short crust pastry as above.
  2 Place flan ring on a greased baking sheet.
  3 Roll out pastry to ¼–½ cm thick and 5 cm larger than flan
    ring.
  4 Lift pastry on the rolling pin; transfer to the ring,
    placing pastry flat on baking sheet.
  5 Gently ease pastry out to corners of flan ring making sure
    there is no air under pastry.
  6 Ease pastry up sides of flan ring without pulling or
    stretching.
  7 Using finger or handle of knife press pastry gently but
    firmly into each flute of the ring.
  8 Roll across top of the flan ring with the rolling pin to
    remove the surplus pastry.
  9 Lightly prick pastry on base of ring.
 10 Place a circle of greaseproof paper on top of the pastry
    and put a layer of baking beans (peas, breadcrusts,
    macaroni, rice, etc.) on the paper.
 11 Bake for about 15 mins. and remove the paper and

beans, and return to the oven for further 10 mins. to dry out.

12 Remove flan ring and place flan carefully on cooling tray. Fill as required.

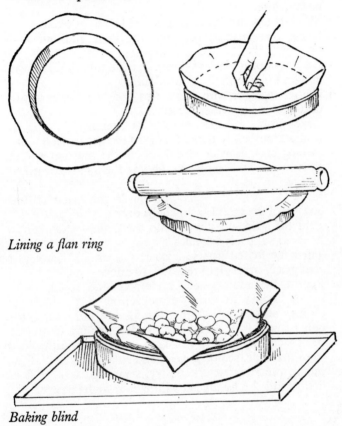

Lining a flan ring

Baking blind

FLAKY OR ROUGH PUFF PASTRY

BASIC RECIPE

200 g strong plain flour　　*75 g lard*
1 level teasp. salt　　　　*75 g margarine*
Few drops lemon juice or　*125 ml water approximately*
pinch of cream of tartar

FLAKY PASTRY

1 Oven 425°F/Gas Mark 7–8.
2 Sieve flour and salt into a mixing bowl with cream of tartar if used.
3 Mix fats together on plate and divide into quarters.
4 Using one quarter, rub into the flour and salt until mixture looks like fine breadcrumbs.
5 Add most of water and lemon juice to mix to soft elastic dough, using a round-bladed knife.
6 Gather together with finger tips and knead very lightly until cracks have disappeared.
7 Cover pastry and allow to relax for 20 mins.
8 Roll out on lightly floured table to rectangle, three times as long as it is wide and 1 cm thick; making sure all corners are right angles and pulling them to shape gently if necessary.
9 Mark the strip of pastry into thirds and using another quarter of the fat, place in knobs over ⅔ of the pastry.
10 Fold the strip into three, with the plain section inside. Press edges firmly to seal.
11 Turn the folded pastry, a quarter turn, and leave in a cool place, covered, to relax for 20 mins.
12 Repeat the addition of fat, folding and rolling twice more, leaving to relax before rolling it to shape. (4 rollings altogether). During the folding and rolling, use only enough flour on the table and rolling pin to prevent the pastry sticking. If it should stick underneath, lift it from the table, scrape it clear, and re-flour lightly. If the rolling pin sticks to the pastry, scrape it clear, re-flour lightly and also lightly pat a little flour to the pastry.

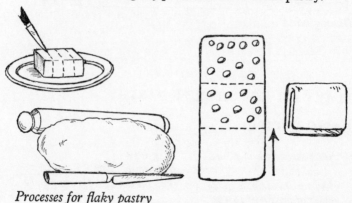

Processes for flaky pastry

ROUGH PUFF PASTRY

1 Oven 425°–450°F/Gas Mark 7–8.
2 Sieve flour and salt together into mixing bowl.
3 Making sure fat is cold and firm, cut into pieces into the flour—making sure each is coated with flour.
4 Add the lemon juice and most of the water and mix to a soft elastic dough, using a round bladed knife. Try not to break up the pieces of fat.
5 Knead gently together with the finger tips.
6 Turn on to a floured table and roll into an oblong three times as long as it is wide and 1 cm thick. Make sure all corners are right angles, pull gently into shape if necessary.
7 Fold the strip into three, seal the edges as for flaky pastry. *N.B.* There is no more fat to add before folding the pastry.

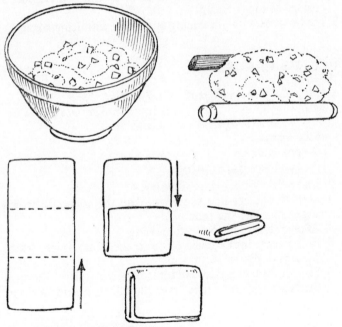

Processes for rough puff pastry

8 Repeat the folding and rolling and leave to relax for 20 mins. before rolling again. (Roll 4 times altogether.)
   Flaky or Rough Puff Pastry may be used in the following ways:

VANILLA SLICES

200 g flaky or rough puff pastry
Confectioner's custard or mock cream, or 125 ml fresh double cream

100 g raspberry jam
Glacé icing or icing sugar for dredging

1 Oven 425°F/Gas Mark 7.
2 Make flaky or rough puff pastry.
3 Roll to a 30 cm square.
4 Trim edges off. Cut into three strips 10 cm long and mark into fingers 3 cm wide.
5 Place strips on to damp baking tray.
6 Bake until firm and golden brown—about 10–12 mins.
7 Cool the pastry, cutting the pieces of pastry apart.
8 Spread jam on half the fingers and then sandwich the pairs together with a thick layer of cream, confectioner's custard or mock cream.
9 Ice the tops with glacé icing or dredge with icing sugar.

ECCLES CAKES

200 g flaky or rough puff pastry
50 g butter or margarine
100 g currants
50 g brown sugar

50 g chopped peel
1 egg white or milk
Caster sugar

1 Oven 425°F/Gas Mark 7.
2 Make flaky or rough puff pastry.
3 Melt the butter in a saucepan. Add the currants, brown sugar and peel and mix.
4 Allow mixture to cool before using.
5 Roll pastry into square or rectangle ½ cm thick. Make squares of pastry 10 cm square.
6 Place a little of mixture in centre of each square. Dampen the edges and draw them over the filling, making a circle.

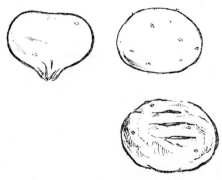

Eccles cakes—shaping and finishing

7 Turn the cake over, roll out so fruit is just visible, keeping circular shape. Make three slits in top of each one.
8 Place on damp baking sheet and bake for 15 mins., top shelf.
9 Brush over with beaten egg white or milk. Sprinkle with caster sugar and return to oven for further 5 mins. for glaze to set.
10 Cool on wire tray.

CREAM HORNS

200 g flaky or rough puff pastry
1 egg beaten
50 g raspberry jam

125 ml double cream or mock cream
Icing sugar

1 Oven 425°F/Gas Mark 7. Grease cream horn tins.
2 Make flaky or rough puff pastry.
3 Roll pastry into oblong, 20 cm x 25 cm.
4 Cut strips of pastry 2 cm wide and brush one edge with beaten egg.
5 Roll a strip on to horn tin, starting at the pointed end. Overlap each new turn of the pastry.
6 Place on damp baking sheet with the end of the pastry underneath.
7 Brush with beaten egg.
8 Bake for 20 mins. on top shelf of heated oven.
9 Remove horn tins and cool on wire tray.
10 Place small teaspoonful of jam in bottom of each cream horn and fill with cream. This can be piped in if desired.
11 Dredge with icing sugar.

Making a cream horn

JAM PUFFS

200 g flaky or rough puff
pastry
100 g jam

1 egg white or milk
Caster sugar

1 Oven 425°F/Gas Mark 7.
2 Make flaky or rough puff pastry.
3 Roll pastry to an oblong or square ½ cm thick.
4 Cut into squares approximately 10 cm.
5 Place jam on each.
6 Brush edges with beaten egg white or milk. Fold pastry over jam to form a triangle. Seal edges firmly.
7 Place on damp baking sheet.

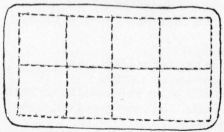

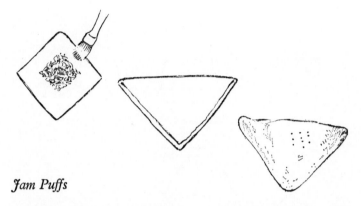

Jam Puffs

8 Brush tops with egg white or milk and sprinkle with caster sugar.
9 Bake in top of pre-heated oven for 15–20 mins.
10 Cool on wire tray.

SAVOURY TRICORNES

200 g flaky or rough puff pastry
Approximately 100–150 g of any savoury filling, e.g.
grated cheese and grated onion
shrimps in white sauce
chicken in white sauce
mushrooms in white sauce
smoked haddock in cheese sauce
Beaten egg white or milk
Parsley for garnish

1 Oven 425°F/Gas Mark 7.
2 Make flaky or rough puff pastry.
3 Make filling—to a thick consistency.
4 Roll pastry out to $\frac{1}{4}$–$\frac{1}{2}$ cm thick.
5 Using a 10 cm plain cutter, cut into circles.
6 Place teaspoonful of mixture in centre of each one and damp the edges of the pastry with beaten egg white or milk.
7 Draw edges of pastry over filling into a three-cornered shape or tricorne.
8 Seal firmly. Brush with beaten egg or milk.
9 Place on damp baking sheet and bake on top shelf of heated oven for 15–20 mins. until firm and golden brown.
10 Cool on wire tray.
11 Serve garnished with parsley.

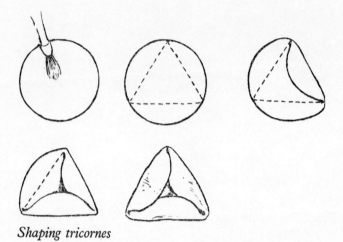

Shaping tricornes

CHOUX PASTRY

ECLAIRS

75 g plain flour
50 g margarine
125 mls water
Pinch each of salt and sugar

2 eggs
150 g icing (chocolate or coffee)
or melted chocolate (see icings)

1 Oven 425°F./Gas Mark 7. Grease a baking sheet and prepare a 2 cm plain savoy tube and a forcing bag. Sieve flour into a piece of greaseproof paper.
2 Place the margarine, water, sugar and salt in a saucepan. Heat slowly until the margarine has melted. Bring to the boil.
3 Whilst still boiling add the flour to the liquid, beating over the heat till the mixture comes away from the sides of the pan and forms a smooth ball. This is a panada.
4 Cool the panada to blood heat. Test with the little finger.
5 Beat the eggs into the panada one at a time until well mixed. Continue beating until the mixture is smooth and elastic, stretching easily from the spoon.
6 Put the mixture into a piping bag. Pipe into a greased tray in 6–7 cm lengths, cutting off with a round bladed knife.
7 Cook 30–40 mins. until golden brown and crisp at the sides. Do not open the oven door for the first 30 minutes. Cool.

Piping cream into éclairs

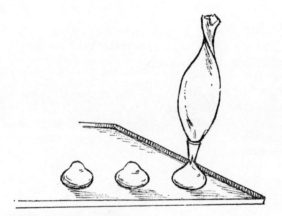

Piping choux pastry

Coating éclairs with chocolate

8 Fill with whipped cream and top with chocolate or coffee icing or melted chocolate.

To make choux buns, proceed as above but pipe the mixture in balls about 5 cm. in diameter.

A larger quantity of éclairs may be made using the following quantities:

125 g plain flour   *Pinch of salt and sugar*
75 g margarine   *3 eggs*
250 mls water

SUET PASTRY

BASIC RECIPE

200 g self-raising flour   *100 g shredded suet*
1 level teasp. salt   *Approximately 125 ml water*

1 Sieve flour and salt into mixing bowl.
2 Mix in the suet.
3 Add enough water to mix to soft elastic dough, using a round bladed knife.
4 Knead to mix all dry flour in and leave bowl clean, and mixture smooth.
5 Use as required.

DUMPLINGS (accompaniment to stew)

1 Make half the quantity suet pastry as above.
2 Divide into eight pieces.
3 Knead to good round shape which will not crack. Cover with flour to help keep shape.
4 Either place in stew 15 mins. from end of cooking time or place in pan of gently boiling salt water. Cover and allow to simmer gently for 15 mins.

16

Batters

YORKSHIRE PUDDING

100 g plain strong flour   *250 ml milk*
¼ teasp. salt   *25 g lard or dripping*
1 egg

1 Oven 425°F/Gas Mark 7.
2 Sift flour and salt. Make a well in the flour.
3 Crack in the egg, add some of the milk and beat till smooth. Add the rest of the milk.
4 Put the fat into a Yorkshire pudding tin or into individual Yorkshire pudding tins. Heat in the oven till it begins to haze.
5 Pour the batter into the hot fat. Cook 20 mins. individual puddings, ½–¾ hour for a large one, till risen and golden brown and crisp. Divide into pieces. Serve at once on an oval plate or around roast beef.

BATTER PUDDING

As above, but serve with jam or syrup as a pudding.

DROPPED FRUIT PUDDING is made by adding black-berries or slices of apple or rhubarb to the tins with the batter, serve with sugar.

PANCAKES

Lard to fry   *250 ml Yorkshire pudding*
Caster sugar   *batter as above*
Orange or lemon juice   *Lemon wedges for serving*

1 Prove a small frying pan by heating a knob of lard until

smoking, pour away, or in the same way as for omelets p. 69.

2 Prepare a piece of paper, sprinkle with caster sugar. Prepare the orange or lemon juice, put the batter in a jug.

3 Melt a small piece of lard in the pan. When it hazes, pour in just enough of the batter to coat the bottom of the pan. Tip the pan to give an even coating.

4 Cook until the mixture sets and comes away from the pan. The edges may be loosened with a palette knife.

5 Toss or turn with a palette knife. Cook the second side till golden brown.

6 Turn on to a sugared paper. Sprinkle with sugar, pour juice over. Roll up with a fork and spoon. Serve on a hot plate with lemon wedges. To keep hot, turn the pancakes from the pan on to a plate over boiling water. Cover with a saucepan lid.

FRITTERS

50 g plain flour
Pinch salt
2 teasp. olive oil
3–4 tablesp. water

1 egg white
3 apples (eating) or 3 bananas or drained pineapple rings

1 Mix the flour, salt, oil and water to a smooth batter. This will coat the back of a spoon. This may be left to stand if wished.

2 Whisk the egg white till stiff. Fold into the batter. Use immediately.

3 Heat the fat in a deep pan (to brown bread in 40 secs.).

4 Put absorbent paper on a baking sheet.

5 Coat the fruit in the batter, holding with two forks. Place in the hot fat. Turn frequently till golden brown and crisp.

6 Turn on to the absorbent paper. Dredge with caster sugar. Serve immediately.

ECONOMICAL COATING BATTER

50 g S.R. flour
Pinch pepper

$\frac{1}{4}$ teasp. salt
4 tablesp. milk or water

1 Blend ingredients to a smooth paste. Use immediately. Suitable for fish or onion rings.

TOAD IN THE HOLE

500 g sausages or sausage   *250 ml Yorkshire pudding*
meat   *batter*

1 Oven 425°F/Gas Mark 7.
2 Prick the sausages if they have skins (divide sausage meat into pieces). Place in a Yorkshire pudding tin. Cook 10 mins to remove some fat. Meanwhile make the batter.
3 Pour the batter over the sausages. Cook 30 mins. till risen and golden. Divide into pieces. Serve immediately, on an oval plate.

17

Beverages

TEA (4 persons)

Water
5 level teasp. tea
Milk and sugar

Allow 1 level teasp. tea per person and 1 teasp. for the pot. Allow 250 ml water per person

1 Place water in kettle. Heat until boiling.
2 Use some of the water to scald the teapot by pouring boiling water into the teapot and pouring away immediately.
3 Return kettle to heat. Bring water back to the boil.
4 Place tea in the pot. Pour boiling water over the tea (this is usually measured by the size of teapot used). Cover with a tea cosy if liked.
5 Pour remaining water into a warm jug.
6 Leave tea to brew for 2–3 mins.
7 Serve with milk and sugar.

COFFEE

500 ml water
4 rounded tablesp. ground coffee
500 ml milk
Brown sugar

Allow approximately 175 ml of coffee per person, e.g. 500 ml black coffee and 500 ml hot milk = 6 cups

(a) Jug method
1 Fill a kettle with water and place to boil.
2 Have the coffee and milk jugs ready.
3 When the kettle is boiling, fill the coffee pot with boiling water and pour away. Keep the pot hot.
4 Return kettle to heat and re-boil.
5 Place ground coffee in the pot. Pour boiling water over

the coffee stirring all the time. Leave to stand in a warm place for 3–5 mins. Run a spoon over the surface to make the grounds sink.
6 Meanwhile, heat the milk and when boiling pour into the milk pot.
7 Serve milk and coffee with brown sugar.

(b) Percolator method
1 Place ground coffee in the percolator box.
2 Pour cold water into the percolator jug.
3 Immerse box in the water.
4 Place lid on pot. Either plug in or place over a hot plate or gas flame according to type.
5 Heat until the coffee is seen to be dark brown in colour, through the glass lid.
6 Meanwhile heat the milk. Pour into milk jug.
7 Serve coffee from the percolator. Serve milk and brown sugar.

INSTANT COFFEE

500 ml water
4 teasp. instant coffee powder
500 ml milk
Brown sugar

Allow 1 teasp. coffee per person

1 Fill a kettle with water. Place to boil.
2 Heat the milk.
3 Put coffee in the pot.
4 Pour 500 ml boiling water over the coffee.
5 Pour milk in milk jug.
6 Serve with brown sugar.

COCOA

500 ml milk or milk and water
6 level teasp. cocoa
3 level teasp. sugar

Allow 2 level teasp. cocoa and 1 level teasp. sugar to taste, per person. About 125 ml liquid per person

1 Place milk or milk and water over a low heat in a pan.
2 Meanwhile mix cocoa and sugar together. During this time the milk will just be warm.
3 Sprinkle cocoa and sugar on to the milk. Whisk in with a wire whisk or fork over the heat.

4 Bring to the boil. Boil for 1 min.
5 Serve hot in a large jug. Serve extra sugar.

LEMONADE OR ORANGEADE

2 lemons or 2 oranges   *500 ml water*
25 g sugar

1 Scrub the lemons or oranges. Dry.
2 Peel thinly with a vegetable peeler.
3 Place the peel and sugar in a jug.
4 Boil the water. Pour boiling water over the peel. Leave to cool.
5 Squeeze out the juice with a lemon squeezer, put into a jug ready for serving.
6 Strain the cooled water over the juice. Taste, add any further sweetener if necessary. Chill before serving.
7 Slices of lemon or orange may be served with the drink.

N.B. If the drink is required hot, pour hot liquid over the juice. Serve at once.

BLACKCURRANT DRINK

2 tablesp. blackcurrant jam   *1 teasp. lemon juice*
250 ml boiling water

1 Place jam in a jug.
2 Pour boiling water over the jam, stirring all the time to dissolve the jam.
3 Add lemon juice. Taste. Add any further sweetener if necessary.
4 Strain into a heatproof glass.
5 Serve hot.

LEMON BARLEY WATER

15 g patent barley   *Zest ½ lemon*
2 tablesp. cold water   *25 g sugar*
1 lt. boiling water   *Juice 3 lemons*

1 Place barley in a pan with the cold water. Mix to a smooth paste.
2 Gradually add boiling water, stirring all the time.

3 Add grated lemon rind and sugar to the barley water.
4 Add lemon juice to cooled barley water.
5 Taste, add any further sweetener if necessary.
6 Strain into serving jug or glasses.
7 Serve cold.

MILK SHAKE

250 ml chilled milk

1 tablesp. blackcurrant jam	*1 teasp. lemon juice*
or	
1 tablesp. rosehip syrup	*1 teasp. lemon juice*
or	
Juice 1 small orange	*2 teasp. sugar*
or	
2 teasp. chocolate powder	*2 teasp. sugar*

BLACKCURRANT SHAKE

Melt blackcurrant jam with lemon juice in a jug. Gradually add the milk, stirring all the time. Whisk together for 2–3 mins. Strain.

ROSE HIP SHAKE

As above, substituting rose hip juice for jam.

ORANGE SHAKE

Squeeze out the juice of the orange. Place with the sugar in a jug. Continue as above.

CHOCOLATE SHAKE

Place milk in the jug. Sprinkle chocolate powder and sugar into the milk. Whisk until chocolate is thoroughly mixed in about 2–3 mins.
All shakes should be served immediately.

SAVOURY MILK

| $\frac{1}{4}$ *teasp. Marmite,* | *250 ml milk* |
| *Bovril or* $\frac{1}{2}$ *Oxo cube* | |

1 Place the flavouring in a large mug.
2 Heat the milk until it boils.
3 Pour milk into the mug, stirring in the flavouring to ensure that it dissolves.
4 Taste, add any further seasoning if required.
5 Serve hot or cold in the mug.

EGG FLIP

125 ml milk
1 egg
½ teasp. sugar

1 teasp. brandy or sherry
or
2 drops brandy essence

1 Place milk in a pan. Heat it until a skin forms on the surface.
2 Meanwhile separate yolk from white of egg.
3 Beat the egg white until it is stiff and peaky.
4 Add yolk to the steaming milk (make sure the milk is turned off at this point). Beat in well.
5 Fold in the white whilst milk is still hot.
6 Add sugar and flavouring.
7 Serve hot or cold in a long glass with a straw and spoon.

ARROWROOT CUP

2 level teasp. arrowroot
250 ml milk

1 teasp. sugar
1 teasp. brandy or sherry or 2 drops brandy essence

1 Place arrowroot and 1 tablesp. of the milk in a pan. Mix to a smooth paste.
2 Gradually add remaining milk, stirring all the time.
3 Heat milk until it thickens and boils, stirring all the time.
4 Add sugar and flavouring. Taste, add any further sweetener if necessary.
5 Serve hot.

APPLE WATER

2 red apples
25 g sugar

Zest and juice of half a lemon
250 ml water

1 Wash and dry apples. Cut into quarters.
2 Place quartered apples (including skin and core) into a large jug with sugar and lemon rind.
3 Boil water. Add boiling water to apples. Stir well. Leave to cool.
4 Add lemon juice to cooled liquid.
5 Taste. Add any further sweetener if necessary.
6 Strain into a serving jug.
7 Serve chilled.

BEEF TEA

500 g raw lean beef   *Salt and pepper*
500 ml cold water

1 Remove any fat from the meat. Wipe over the meat.
2 Mince beef finely, using a mincer.
3 Place beef and water in a heat-proof jug. Leave to stand for 1 hour.
4 Place jug to stand in a large pan. Add water to the pan half way up the jug.
5 Boil the water 2–3 hours, stirring beef and water in the jug occasionally.
6 Strain beef tea. Season. Taste. Cool.
7 Strain off any fat when cool.
8 Reheat before serving.
9 Serve with additional seasonings, e.g. Worcestershire sauce, thus catering for individual tastes.

18

Salads

A salad is a mixture of almost any vegetables, fruits and nuts. Eating raw vegetables means that the valuable vitamins and mineral salts contained in the vegetables are not lost, and since there is a great variety of salads one should not overlook their value in the diet.

Uses of salads

1 Salads may be used for hors d'oeuvre dishes.
2 They may be used as an accompaniment to a meat, e.g. chicken or steak, or vegetarian dish, e.g. cheese flan. Served in this way they should have a French dressing.
3 The most usual type of salad forms part of a main meal, in which case it must contain some type of complete protein food—either egg, meat, fish or cheese.
4 Buffet parties may also have many different types of salad included, using both cooked and uncooked ingredients. Salads should be served with a salad dressing to enhance the flavour of the vegetables used and to help digestion.

Choice and preparation of suitable ingredients

Vegetable	Choice	Preparation
Beetroot	Should be deep red in colour and free from soil, with fresh leaves. Treat with care to prevent bruising, which may cause loss of colour.	For cooking see vegetables, p. 76. Cooked beetroot should be skinned and cooled, sliced or diced. Serve with or without vinegar.

Brussels sprouts	Choose firm closed sprouts with undamaged leaves and no discoloration.	Remove any outer damaged leaves. Wash carefully, shred finely.
Cabbage	Choose firm hearts	Use the white heart only. Wash, drain and shred finely.
Carrot	Should be firm and free from soil	Wash, peel or scrape or scrub as necessary. Grate. Arrange on salad in heaps.
Cauliflower	Do not buy those which are discoloured, but those which are a creamy white in colour. They should feel firm and be surrounded with fresh green leaves.	Slice off any bad or discoloured parts. Wash thoroughly and divide into tiny florets. May also be used chopped.
Celery	Should be white in colour. Leaves should look fresh and crisp. Thick stalks are tough.	Separate stalks and scrub. Either cut into $\frac{1}{2}$ cm pieces or into dice or shredded lengthways and left in cold water to curl.
Chicory	Should be firm and undamaged.	Remove any damaged parts. Wash. Leaves should be left whole or halved lengthways, or cut in thick slices.
Cucumber	Should have dark green skin and be firm. If buying half a cucumber, the cut should show the inside to be a good white colour. Now	Wash the skin. Remove one thick slice and discard. Slice the rest very thinly. Marks may be made in the skin of the cucumber

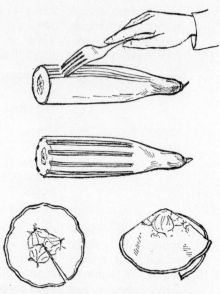

Above: *methods of decorating cucumber;* below: *cucumber slice folded over*

	often pre-packed in plastic.	using a fork, for added decoration. The skin may be removed altogether, depending on personal taste.
Endive	Has very curly dark green outer leaves with a yellowy centre. The outer leaves may be rather coarse.	Remove outer leaves. Wash under cold running water. Drain and dry in salad basket, or cloth.
Lettuce	There are two main types available. Cos, which has long leaves, and Round which has a good firm heart. Discoloration of the	Separate leaves, removing any damaged parts. Always handle carefully to prevent further damage and gently tear damaged parts

stem indicates the length of time the lettuce has been cut. Do not buy badly bruised or discolored lettuce. Lettuce are often pre-packed in polythene bags.

away. Wash thoroughly and dry carefully. Crisp any limp leaves in the crisper compartment of the refrigerator. Leaves may be used whole or shredded finely with a very sharp knife to prevent loss of Vitamin C from the damaged cell walls.

Mushrooms	Button mushrooms. Skins not discoloured.	Peel if necessary. Wash and dry. Slice or chop.
Mustard and Cress	Grown in small plastic or card containers and will therefore keep for a few days more than most salad ingredients, if watered, but not too long otherwise it becomes very strong in flavour.	For use as garnish, wash by tilting container under tap. Cut off in bunches level with container top. Use as garnish. For use in salads wash after cutting, using a sieve or colander.
Peppers (pimentoes) green or red	Should be unbruised and crisp.	Remove stalk, top and seeds. Wash and slice.

Preparing green peppers

Radishes	Bought in bunches. The size can vary considerably—large ones becoming hollow and woody in texture.	Remove leaves and root. Wash all soil away carefully. The radish may be left whole or sliced thinly. Roses may be made by cutting the radishes. If prepared in these two ways, they should then be left to stand in a basin of cold water to 'open out'. This takes about 30 mins.
Spinach	Should be dark green in colour and not limp.	Needs to be washed most carefully to remove all traces of grit. Remove coarse veins. Shred. For cooking method, see p. 74.
Spring Onions	Bought by the bunch. The larger the onion the stronger the flavour.	Cut off roots and the tough dark tops, leaving each onion about 8 cm long. Peel off outer layer and wash carefully.

Water lily tomatoes

Tomatoes	Choose even sized firm tcmatoes which are a good red colour. The stalk indicates the freshness of the tomato.	Skin—see cooking terms p. 16 to blanch. Alternatively, rotate for a few secs. in a gas flame until the skin splits after popping.
Turnip or Swede	Choose young ones which have a delicate flavour.	Peel thickly and grate.
Watercress	Bought in bunches. Should have dark green leaves and white rootlets along the stems. Avoid buying those bunches with damaged leaves or thick, coarse stalks.	Remove damaged leaves, coarse stalks and rootlets. Wash in at least 2 changes of cold salt water to remove any grubs.

Some vegetables may be used cooked and cold, such as beetroot, broad beans, French or runner beans, carrots, cauliflower, celery, mushrooms, peas, potatoes and turnip.
Fruits and nuts which may be used are apples, bananas, dates, grapes, grapefruit, oranges, pineapples, raisins, sultanas and walnuts.
The fruits are prepared as for fruit salads.
Herbs used for flavouring are chives, mint, parsley and others to personal taste.

Rules for making salads
1 Use really fresh vegetables which are in good condition.
2 Handle as little as possible.
3 Prepare and wash as described.
4 Drain to remove surplus water either on a clean cloth, or sieve, or colander, or cake cooling tray.
5 Vegetables which need crisping may be placed in the crisper of a refrigerator for 30 mins. before using.
6 Use leaves whole or shredded finely with a sharp knife.
7 Do not have too many flavours or colours in a salad, otherwise they look very untidy and unappetizing.
8 Prepare all ingredients before beginning to mix or arrange.

9 Save some ingredients for decoration.
10 Always serve a salad dressing.

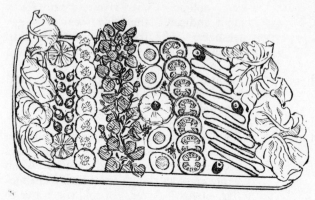

Arrangement of a salad

Salads used as Hors d'oeuvres

BEETROOT

1 Use cooked and diced, with spiced vinegar or French dressing and garnished with chopped green herbs.
2 Always serve separately, since other vegetables will be discoloured.

CELERY

1 Wash and scrape and curl as directed.
2 Chill before serving.

CUCUMBER

1 Slice thinly.
2 Arrange neatly in dish.
3 Coat with French dressing or spiced vinegar.
4 Garnish with chopped parsley.

POTATO SALAD

250–500 g new potatoes.   *Salad cream or mayonnaise to*
Cooked potatoes may be used *coat*
1–2 chopped spring onions or *Seasoning*
1 tablesp. chopped chives   *Parsley or mint for garnish*

1 If potatoes are uncooked, scrape them and boil in salt water until tender.
2 Drain and cool slightly.
3 Cut into slices or neat dice.
4 Chop onions or chives and mix with dressing.
5 Add potatoes and mix carefully. Season to taste.
6 Serve garnished with chopped mint or parsley.

TOMATO SALAD

1 Skin and slice few tomatoes thinly.
2 Arrange neatly in dish. Coat with French dressing.
3 Garnish with chopped parsley.

CREAM CHEESE AND PINEAPPLE SALAD (1)

Few lettuce leaves   *25 g cream cheese per person*
1 ring pineapple for each per- *25 g chopped walnuts*
son

1 Wash and drain lettuce. Arrange on tea plate— approximately 2 leaves per person.
2 Arrange ring of pineapple on top.
3 Make each 25 g cream cheese into ball by wetting hands first and rolling between palms.
4 Coat each with chopped nuts and place in centre of each pineapple ring.

CREAM CHEESE AND PINEAPPLE SALAD (2)

1 Chop four rings of pineapple and mix with about 75 g cream cheese.
2 Place in dish. Garnish with tomato.

There are many other vegetables which may be served separately as components of an hors d'oeuvre tray.

Main meals

ENGLISH SALAD OR SUMMER SALAD

This can be a combination of almost any salad vegetables, usually limited to about 4 or 5 to keep it simple and yet attractive.

Lettuce	*Tomatoes*
Watercress	*Radishes*
Mustard and cress	*Spring onions*
Cucumber	*Carrot*

1 Prepare vegetables according to kind.
2 Shred lettuce. Use as a basis to the salad. Serve on oval or round plate for ease of serving.
3 Arrange other vegetables geometrically and attractively. Always leave enough plate clear to allow it to be passed around when serving.
4 Serve as soon as possible after preparation with a salad dressing.

N.B. To serve as a main dish add protein in the form of eggs, cheese or meat.

FRENCH OR TOSSED SALAD

Usually consists of only 1 or 2 of the salad ingredients tossed in French dressing, served in a bowl and served as accompaniment to fried chicken portions or grilled steak, e.g.

1 Lettuce and chopped chives and French dressing.
2 Endive with French dressing.
3 Any of the salads used as hors d'oeuvre.

GREEN SALADS WITH FRUIT

Fruit can be incorporated in salads to give a fresh taste to what otherwise may be a rather uninteresting and uncolourful salad. Serve with French dressing or salad cream.

1 Lettuce, watercress and grapefruit or orange segments.
2 Lettuce, celery and orange segments.
3 Lettuce, chicory, banana, grapes and chopped nuts.
4 Endive, chopped apple, dates and raisins.

WINTER SALAD

½ *white cabbage heart*	*Chopped parsley*
1 raw carrot	*2 tablesp. French dressing*
1 celery heart	*Garnish—sliced tomato or*
2 tablesp. raisins	*carrot*

1 Prepare all ingredients according to kind.
2 Mix lightly together.
3 Toss in French dressing.
4 Arrange in bowl and garnish with a colourful ingredient such as carrot or tomato if available.

N.B. Other vegetables which may be used for winter salads in any combination desired are:

Boiled beetroot	*Watercress*
Apples	*Cauliflower*
Walnuts	*Turnip*
Tinned or cooked peas	*Sprouts*

RUSSIAN SALAD

A combination of cooked vegetables, e.g. carrot, beetroot, swede, peas, mushrooms tossed in mayonnaise or salad cream.

Buffet Salads (quantities may be increased to suit the number of people being served)

RICE SALAD

100 g Patna rice	½ *red or green pepper*
2 tomatoes	*50 g cooked peas*
cucumber	*raisins (optional)*
celery	*cooked ham or chicken*
1 onion	*Seasoning*
15 g margarine	*Paprika pepper*

1 Boil rice in salted water till soft (10 minutes).
2 Rinse in cold water. Drain well.
3 Dry rice slowly.
4 Place in mixing bowl.
5 Meanwhile, prepare other ingredients.
6 Blanch and chop tomatoes, chop cucumber and celery.
7 Peel and chop onion and fry in margarine until soft (may be left raw).

8 Remove stalk and seeds from pepper. Blanch if wished. Slice or dice.
9 Place all prepared ingredients in mixing bowl, also the dried rice, together with seasoning and paprika.
10 Mix lightly together. Taste and alter seasoning if necessary.
11 Serve in a clean dish.

N.B. Not all the above ingredients may be liked—if so, omit or alter as necessary.

OTHER SALADS FOR BUFFETS

These are usually arranged on large trays. The ingredients are various combinations of any of the following:

Sausages such as Strasbourg, Lyons, Frankfurt, Salami, Bologna, Saveloy, all served thinly sliced garnished with parsley.
Smoked ham, tongue, chicken or game.
Shell fish, anchovies, sardines, salmon.
Hard boiled egg. Cheeses.

Vegetables
Lettuce, chicory, endive, watercress, cress, cabbage hearts, sprouts, carrots, beetroot, radish, celery, cauliflower, tomatoes.

These are all prepared according to type and arranged in neat rows along the trays, making for easy serving.
Suitable salad dressings are also served.

Fruit (see also fresh fruit salad)

APPLES, COOKING

Peel thinly with a vegetable peeler. Remove core, using an apple corer or vegetable peeler.

(1) Cut into quarters. Slice for pies.
(2) Cut into rings for fritters.
(3) Cut into quarters then chunks for stewing.

APPLES, DESSERT (fruit salad)

Wash. Do not peel. Remove core. Slice into rings. Coat in lemon juice. Cut each ring into 6 pieces. Coat cut edges in lemon juice.

APRICOTS

Remove stalk, wash, dry. Cut into quarters, removing the stone.

BANANAS

Skin, slice, coat in lemon juice.

BILBERRIES

Remove stalk. Wash. Shake dry.

BLACKBERRIES, RASPBERRIES, LOGANBERRIES

Remove stalk, wash. Shake dry.

CHERRIES

Remove stalk. Wash and dry. Remove stone with a cherry stoner or cut in half lengthways removing the stone.

DAMSONS

Remove stalk. Wash. Stone and skin if necessary after cooking.

GOOSEBERRIES

Top and tail, wash. Shake dry.

GRAPES

Remove stalk. Wash and dry. Cut in half lengthways. Remove pips.

13—ACB * *

MELON

See hors d'oeuvres.

ORANGES

Peel thinly. Remove pith with a vegetable knife to expose flesh. Halve the orange, divide into segments. Remove pips. Cut each segment into 2 or 3 depending on size. See diagram.

PEACHES

Wash. Cut into quarters removing stone. Slice thinly. Coat in lemon juice.

PEARS

Remove stalk, peel thinly.
(1)   Remove core $\frac{3}{4}$ way up pear for poaching.
(2)   Cut into quarters, remove core for stewing.
(3)   Cut into quarters, remove core. Slice, coat in lemon juice. Cut each slice into 3. Coat cut edges.

PINEAPPLE

Remove stalk and base. Peel thickly. Remove hard core in centre. Slice into rings. Divide each ring into 6 pieces.

PLUMS

Remove stalk. Wash. Cut into half removing stone. Cut in half again for fruit salad.

RHUBARB

Wash. Top and tail. Remove stringy skin. Cut into 1 in. lengths.

STRAWBERRIES

Wash and then remove stalk to preserve flavour. Leave whole or cut in half lengthways depending on size.

19

Sauces, stuffings and salad dressings

Sauces

Roux Sauces

SAVOURY WHITE POURING SAUCE

15 g butter or margarine	*3 shakes pepper*
15 g flour	*½ teasp. salt*
250 ml milk (125 ml milk +	
125 ml white stock may be	
used)	

1 Melt fat in a small pan. Do not overheat or the fat will burn and give the sauce a bitter flavour.
2 Add flour over heat. Mix to a smooth paste with the fat using a wooden spoon.
3 Cook the roux for 1–2 mins., stirring all the time to prevent it from sticking to the pan. Do not brown the roux.
4 Add liquid a little at a time away from the heat. Do not add too much liquid at once, otherwise it will not mix in easily with the roux.
5 Return pan to the heat. Heat the sauce, stirring all the time, until it thickens and boils. Cook for a further 2 mins. to ensure that the starch is thoroughly cooked, otherwise the sauce will have a powdery flavour.
6 Add seasoning. Taste. Add any further seasoning if necessary.
7 Serve immediately in a sauce boat.

N.B. If any sauce must be kept hot cover the surface of the sauce with wet greaseproof paper to prevent a skin forming, and keep in a warm place.

Variations of a pouring sauce

ANCHOVY SAUCE

Use 125 ml milk and 125 ml fish stock. Add 1 tablesp. chopped anchovies or 2 teasp. anchovy essence, and 2 teasp. lemon juice during the 2 mins. cooking of the sauce.

CAPER SAUCE

Use 125 ml milk and 125 ml fish stock or mutton stock (depending on what it is to be served with). Add 1 tablesp. chopped capers and 2 teasp. vinegar during the 2 mins. cooking.

CHEESE SAUCE

Use all milk. Add 50 g grated cheese, 1 shake cayenne pepper and 1 teasp. made mustard with the seasonings.

EGG SAUCE

Use all milk. Add 1 chopped hard boiled egg during 2 mins. cooking.

MUSHROOM SAUCE

Fry 50 g finely chopped mushrooms in the melted butter for 10 mins. before adding the flour. Proceed as for white sauce.

MUSTARD SAUCE

Use 125 ml milk and 125 ml beef stock or 125 ml fish stock (depending on what it is to be served with). Add 1 teasp. made mustard during 2 mins. cooking.

ONION SAUCE

Use 125 ml milk and 125 ml onion stock. Add 1 cooked finely chopped onion during 2 mins. cooking.

PARSLEY SAUCE

Use 125 ml milk and 125 ml fish or bacon or ham stock (depending on what it is to be served with). Add 1 tablesp. fresh chopped parsley or 2 teasp. dried parsley during 2 mins. cooking.

SWEET POURING WHITE SAUCE

15 g sugar   *15 g margarine or butter*
250 ml milk   *15 g flour*

1 Dissolve sugar in the milk.
2 Follow method as for savoury white sauce.
3 Taste, add any further sweetener if necessary.

Variations of a sweet pouring sauce

BRANDY OR RUM SAUCE

Add 1 tablesp. brandy or rum with the sugar.

COFFEE OR CHOCOLATE SAUCE

Add 2 teasp. chocolate powder or coffee essence with the sugar. Add colouring if necessary.

ORANGE OR LEMON SAUCE

Add rind and juice of one orange or one lemon after the sauce has thickened. Reheat sauce.

WHITE COATING SAUCE

25 g margarine or butter   *250 ml milk*
25 g flour

Savoury: *Sweet:*
3 shakes pepper   *15 g sugar*
½ teasp. salt

1 Follow method for pouring sauce. This sauce when completed should be thick enough to coat the back of a wooden spoon.

2 Additional flavourings may be used as for pouring sauce.
3 Coating sauces are usually poured over the food they are served with, as opposed to being served separately, e.g. cauliflower cheese.

PANADA SAUCE

50 g margarine or butter   250 ml milk
50 g flour
Savoury: Sweet:
  3 shakes pepper   15 g sugar
  ½ teasp. salt

1 Follow method as for pouring sauce. This sauce will be extremely thick. Thick enough to stand a spoon in it.
2 Additional flavourings may be added but a greater quantity will be required than for pouring sauce, e.g. double quantity of additional flavouring should be used, 100 g mushrooms for mushroom panada; 100 g chicken for chicken panada; 50 g cheese for cheese panada; 2 hard boiled eggs for egg panada.
3 Panadas are used as fillings for patties, or for binding, e.g. fish cakes.

BROWN SAUCE

1 small carrot   250 ml brown stock
½ small onion   ¼ teasp. salt
15 g dripping   3 shakes pepper
15 g flour   ½ teasp. beef extract

1 Peel and grate carrot and onion.
2 Melt dripping in a pan. Lightly fry vegetables in the fat.
3 Add flour over the heat, mix to a smooth paste. Cook the roux, stirring all the time, until golden brown.
4 Add stock a little at a time as for white sauce.
5 Return to heat. Heat the sauce until it thickens and boils, stirring all the time.
6 Add seasonings and beef extract. Cook for 2 mins.
7 Taste, add any further seasoning and a little gravy browning or gravy salt if necessary.
8 Strain into a sauce boat. Serve at once (it may be kept hot as for white sauce).

BROWN GRAVY

2 tablesp. meat juices and
dripping
1 rounded tablesp. flour

250 ml vegetable stock
Salt and pepper

1 After removing meat and straining off the fat from roasting meat, leave 2 tablesp. juices and dripping in the roasting tin.
2 Heat fat until it is just smoking.
3 Add flour, mix to a smooth paste. Brown and cook roux as for brown sauce.
4 Add vegetable stock as for brown sauce.
5 Heat gravy until it thickens and boils. Add seasoning.
6 Taste, add any further seasoning or colouring if necessary.
7 Strain into a sauce boat. Serve as for brown sauce.

MAITRE D'HOTEL SAUCE

25 g butter or margarine
15 g flour
250 ml milk

1 tablesp. finely chopped
parsley
½ teasp. salt
3 shakes pepper

1 Melt fat in a pan.
2 Add flour over the heat. Whisk in the fat to a smooth paste with the flour.
3 Add milk away from heat as for white sauce.
4 Heat until it thickens and boils. Add parsley and seasoning. Cook for 2 mins.
5 Taste and serve as for white sauce.

BECHAMEL SAUCE

½ small carrot
½ small onion
1 stick celery
1 bay leaf
6 peppercorns
Piece blade mace
½ teasp. salt

3 shakes pepper
250 ml milk
15 g margarine or butter
15 g flour
2 tablesp. cream or top of
milk

1 Peel and slice vegetables. Place vegetables, seasoning, herbs and milk in a pan.
2 Bring milk to the boil. Leave to stand for 30 mins.

3 Melt fat. Add flour over the heat. Mix to a smooth paste. Cook roux as for white sauce.
4 Strain milk. Add to roux as for white sauce.
5 Heat sauce until it thickens and boils. Cook for 2 mins. Turn off heat.
6 Add cream. Stir into sauce.
7 Taste, season if necessary.
8 Serve as for white sauce.

DUTCH OR MOCK HOLLANDAISE SAUCE

250 ml Béchamel sauce (as   *2 tablesp. cream*
above without cream)   *2 teasp. lemon juice*
1 egg yolk

1 Prepare Béchamel sauce without cream.
2 Mix cream and egg yolk together.
3 Add lemon juice to thickened sauce. Mix well.
4 Turn off the heat. Add cream and egg mixture. Mix well.
5 Turn heat on. Cook the sauce once more without boiling. Boiling will cause egg and cream to curdle.
6 Serve in a sauce boat immediately. This sauce cannot be kept hot.

Blending Sauces

SAVOURY WHITE BLENDING SAUCE

15 g cornflour   *½ teasp. salt*
250 ml milk   *Optional—knob of margarine*
3 shakes pepper

1 Place cornflour and 2 tablesp. milk in a pan. Blend to a smooth paste.
2 Gradually add the remaining liquid a little at a time. Add margarine.
3 Heat sauce, gently stirring all the time, until it thickens and boils. Cook for 2 mins.
4 Add seasoning. Taste, add any further seasoning if necessary.
5 Serve hot in a sauce boat.

Variations
Savoury flavourings as for white roux sauce may be added during the 2 mins. cooking of the sauce. The same quantities as suggested for the roux sauce should be used.

SWEET BLENDING SAUCE

15 g cornflour   *15 g sugar*
250 ml milk or fruit juice (and
water to make up quantity)

See method as for savoury sauce. Dissolve sugar in the liquid.

Variations

ORANGE OR LEMON SAUCE

Use juice and rind of one orange or lemon. Replace some of the liquid with the fruit juice but keep separately. Add orange or lemon juice and rind during 2 mins. cooking.

COFFEE SAUCE

Add 2 teasp. coffee essence to the cornflour. Mix both to a smooth paste with the milk.

BUTTERSCOTCH SAUCE

100 g brown sugar   *Rind and juice of ½ lemon*
250 ml water or milk   *15 g cornflour*
25 g butter

1 Dissolve the sugar in 125 ml of the water or milk by heating gently and stirring.
2 Add butter and lemon rind, boil for 5 mins.
3 Place cornflour in a basin with 2 tablesp. of remaining liquid.
4 Blend to a smooth paste. Gradually add the remaining liquid.
5 Gradually add the made syrup mixture.
6 Heat sauce until it thickens and boils. Cook for 2 mins. Add lemon juice.
7 Taste. Add any further sweetener if necessary.
8 Serve in a sauce boat.

CARAMEL SAUCE

50 g golden syrup   *250 ml milk*

1 tablesp. warm water   *15 g cornflour*
2 drops vanilla essence

1 Heat syrup gently in a clean dry pan until it is deep brown in colour.
2 Add warm water (blood heat) at once. Leave syrup (caramel) to cool.
3 Add vanilla to the milk.
4 Blend cornflour and 2 tablesp. of milk to a smooth paste in a basin.
5 Gradually add the remaining milk.
6 Add milk mixture over a low heat a little at a time to the caramel in order to dissolve it. Gently stir the mixture as the milk is being added.
7 Heat sauce, stirring all the time, until it thickens and boils. Cook for 2 mins.
8 Taste. Serve in a sauce boat.

CHOCOLATE SAUCE

60 g plain chocolate   *15 g cornflour*
250 ml milk or water   *15 g sugar*

1 Grate chocolate, place in a basin with 2 tablesp. of the liquid.
2 Melt chocolate over hot water (see icings).
3 Blend cornflour and another 2 tablesp. of liquid to a smooth paste in a small pan.
4 Gradually add remaining liquid and sugar.
5 Heat sauce, stirring all the time until it thickens and boils. Cook for 2 mins.
6 Add warmed melted chocolate. Stir in well.
7 Taste. Serve in a sauce boat.

GINGER SAUCE

15 g cornflour   *1 tablesp. golden syrup*
250 ml milk   *½ teasp. ground ginger*
15 g sugar   *1–2 teasp. lemon juice*

1 Follow method as for sweet blending sauce.
2 Add syrup and ginger when sauce is boiling. Add lemon juice. Re-heat sauce, stirring all the time.
3 Serve in a sauce boat.

CUSTARD SAUCE

15 g custard powder   *250 ml milk*
25 g sugar

1 Place custard powder, sugar and 2 tablesp. of milk in a basin. Blend to a smooth paste.
2 Boil remaining milk.
3 Add boiling milk to custard powder paste, stirring all the time.
4 Rinse pan. Return sauce to pan.
5 Heat until it thickens and boils. Cook for 2 mins. Serve in a sauce boat.

TOMATO SAUCE

15 g cornflour   *½ teasp. sugar*
250 ml canned tomato juice   *Grated nutmeg*
Seasoning   *1 teasp. lemon juice*

1 Place cornflour in a pan. Blend to a smooth paste with 1 tablesp. of the juice.
2 Gradually add remaining liquid a little at a time.
3 Add seasoning, sugar and nutmeg.
4 Heat sauce until it thickens and boils. Cook for 2 mins.
5 Add lemon juice. Taste. Add any further seasonings if required.
6 Serve hot in a sauce boat.

FRUIT SAUCES

Fruit sauce   *10 g arrowroot*
250 ml fruit juice from tin of *2 tablesp. diced fruit*
fruit   *Sugar (optional)*

1 Place arrowroot in a pan with 1 tablesp. of the fruit juice. Blend to a smooth paste.
2 Gradually add remaining juice a little at a time.
3 Add diced fruit.
4 Heat sauce, stirring all the time until it thickens and boils. Cook for 2 mins.
5 Add lemon juice. Taste. Add sugar if necessary.
6 Serve in a sauce boat.

JAM OR MARMALADE SAUCE

250 ml water
10 g arrowroot
2 tablesp. jam or marmalade

1–2 teasp. lemon juice
Sugar to sweeten if necessary

1 Place jam or marmalade and water in a pan. Heat gently, stirring all the time, until jam or marmalade has just melted. The liquid should only be warm at this stage.
2 Place arrowroot in a basin. Blend to a smooth paste with 1 tablesp. of the jam liquid. Gradually add remaining liquid a little at a time.
3 Rinse pan. Return liquid to pan. Heat until it thickens and boils, stirring all the time. Cook for 2 mins.
4 Add lemon juice. Taste. Add sugar if necessary.
5 Strain sauce. Serve in a sauce boat or use as a glaze.

SYRUP SAUCE

250 ml water
10 g arrowroot
2 tablesp. syrup

¼ teasp. ginger
1–2 teasp. lemon juice

See method for jam sauce. Mix ginger with arrowroot. This sauce will not need straining.

Butter Sauces

BRANDY OR RUM BUTTER

75 g icing sugar
50 g butter
3 drops lemon juice
2–4 teasp. brandy or rum

1 drop almond essence
2 drops vanilla essence
Glacé cherries and angelica

1 Sieve icing sugar into a basin.
2 Cream icing sugar and butter together until white and fluffy (see icings).
3 Gradually work in the lemon juice, essences and flavourings.
4 Pipe into a glass dish. Decorate with glacé cherries and angelica.
5 Serve in the dish with a spoon.

MAITRE D'HOTEL BUTTER

25 g butter   *Little cayenne pepper*
1 tablesp. chopped parsley   *Few drops lemon juice*

1 Cream butter in a basin until white and fluffy.
2 Gradually mix in the other ingredients.
3 Form into a neat roll. Wrap in wet greaseproof paper.
  Place in a refrigerator to solidify. Before serving, cut into
  pats or use a butter curler.
4 Serve with grills.

DEVILLED BUTTER

50 g butter   *¼ teasp. dry mustard*
2 teasp. finely chopped pars- *1 tablesp. lemon juice*
ley

As for Maître d'Hôtel Butter.

Miscellaneous Sauces

APPLE SAUCE

250 g cooking apples   *Strip lemon rind*
2 tablesp. water   *15 g margarine*
25 g sugar

1 Place water, margarine, sugar and lemon rind in a pan,
  slowly bring to the boil.
2 Peel, core and slice apples.
3 Place apples in the boiling water. Turn down to simmer.
  Cover pan.
4 Gently stew apples until tender, 5–20 mins. depending on
  type of apples.
5 Test for tenderness with a skewer.
6 Beat apples to pulp.
7 Pass through a sieve.
8 Serve hot in a sauce boat with a spoon.

BREAD SAUCE

1 small onion   *250 ml milk*
1 blade mace   *2 slices bread, 1 cm thick,*
1 bay leaf   *from a large loaf*

2 cloves	*15 g butter*
4 peppercorns	*Salt*

1 Peel and quarter the onion.
2 Place cloves in onion and put in a pan with the milk. Add mace, bayleaf and peppercorns in a muslin bag.
3 Bring milk to the boil. Turn off heat. Cover pan. Leave to stand for 30 mins.
4 Meanwhile grate bread into a large basin.
5 Strain milk over breadcrumbs. Leave to soak for 15 mins. Discard onion and spices.
6 Return bread and milk to pan. Re-heat until it just boils. Stir in the butter. Taste. Add salt if necessary.
7 Serve hot in a sauce boat with a spoon.

CRANBERRY SAUCE

50 g sugar	*125 ml water*
250 g cranberries	

1 Place sugar, cranberries and water in a pan.
2 Bring water to the boil. Turn down to simmer. Cover pan.
3 Stew cranberries until they pop. (It may be necessary to add more water.)
4 Rub through a sieve. Taste, add more sugar if necessary.
5 Serve in a sauce boat with a spoon.

CURRY SAUCE

1 small onion	*25 g desiccated coconut*
1 small cooking apple	*1 teasp. black treacle*
15 g margarine	*1 teasp. mango chutney*
15 g curry powder	*2 teasp. lemon juice*
15 g flour	*25 g sultanas*
250 ml water	

1 Peel and chop the onion finely. Peel and chop the apple coarsely. Apple may be grated if preferred.
2 Melt margarine in a large pan.
3 Fry onion in the fat until it is beginning to soften and brown.
4 Add curry powder. Cook for 5 mins., stirring all the time.
5 Stir in the flour. Add water, apple and coconut. Stir the sauce until it simmers.
6 Add all other ingredients. Simmer the sauce for 1 hour,

stirring occasionally. Simmer until all ingredients are soft, almost at the pulp stage.

7 Serve sauce with cooked meat or hard boiled eggs. Also serve some Patna rice.

MINT SAUCE

2 rounded tablesp. finely chopped mint
2 tablesp. boiling water
1 tablesp. caster sugar
2 tablesp. vinegar

1 Place caster sugar and mint in a small sauce boat.
2 Dissolve caster sugar by pouring the boiling water over it. Leave it to cool.
3 Add vinegar to the cooled liquid. Stir.
4 Serve in the sauce boat with a small spoon at the side.

HORSE-RADISH SAUCE

75 ml top of the milk
2 tablesp. grated horse-radish
2 teasp. vinegar
1 teasp. lemon juice
½ teasp. sugar

1 Mix all the ingredients together in a small basin.
2 Taste. Add any further seasonings if necessary.
3 Serve in a small sauce boat with a spoon.

BARBECUE SAUCE

250 ml canned tomato puree
75 ml vinegar
50 g brown sugar
1 teasp. flaked celery or
½ teasp. celery salt
1 tablesp. Worcestershire sauce
¼ teasp. chilli powder
500 ml water
Tabasco sauce (optional)

1 Place all ingredients in a large pan.
2 Bring water to the boil. Turn down to simmer. Place lid on the pan.
3 Simmer sauce gently for 30 mins.
4 Taste sauce. Tabasco sauce may be added to taste. Add any further seasoning if necessary.
5 Strain into sauce boat. Serve hot.

EGG CUSTARD SAUCE

2 small eggs	*2 teasp. caster sugar*
250 ml milk	*Little vanilla essence*

1 Break eggs in a basin. Beat well with sugar and essence.
2 Heat milk to almost boiling point, when a skin is visible on the surface and milk is bubbling around the sides.
3 Gently pour over the beaten egg, stirring all the time.
4 Rinse pan. Strain sauce into pan. A double saucepan may be used if available.
5 Heat gently (do not boil) until egg tastes cooked and the sauce thickens slightly—enough to coat back of spoon.
6 Serve hot or cold in a sauce boat.

MAYONNAISE SAUCE
See Dressings.

Serving sauces

Sauce	Dish
Anchovy sauce	Fish dishes
Apple sauce	Duck, goose, pork
Barbecue sauce	Meat dishes. Grills
Brandy or Rum sauce	Christmas pudding
Bread sauce	Chicken, turkey
Brown sauce	Meat dishes
Butterscotch sauce	Ice cream
Caper sauce	Fish, mutton
Caramel sauce	Caramel custard or pudding
Cheese sauce	Vegetables, cheese pies, fish dishes
Coffee or chocolate sauce	Coffee or chocolate pudding, ice cream
Cranberry sauce	Turkey
Custard sauce	Puddings and pies
Egg sauce	Fish, vegetables
Fruit sauces	Upside-down pudding, steamed puddings
Jam sauce	Flans, steamed sponges, jam roly poly
Mint sauce	Lamb
Mushroom sauce	Fish and grills
Onion sauce	Mutton

Sauce	Dish
Orange and lemon sauce	Orange and lemon pudding
Parsley sauce	Fish, ham
Syrup sauce	Ginger pudding, baked apples
Tomato sauce	Fish. Pasta dishes

Stuffings

VEAL STUFFING (suitable for all purposes)

50 g breadcrumbs	Grated zest ½ lemon
15 g margarine	Seasoning
1 tablesp. chopped parsley	Beaten egg
½ teasp. mixed herbs	

1 Place breadcrumbs in a large basin.
2 Mash or rub in the margarine.
3 Add herbs and seasoning. Mix.
4 Bind together with beaten egg to a very stiff consistency.

STUFFING BALLS

50 g stuffing mixture	50 g golden breadcrumbs
1 egg	Deep fat for frying

1 Knead stuffing to a smooth ball. Roll into a sausage shape, divide into 8 pieces.
2 Roll each piece into a neat firm ball.
3 Beat the egg well. Pour on to a plate.
4 Place breadcrumbs on a second plate.
5 Place balls in the egg, coat well. Toss in breadcrumbs. Repeat. Shake off any loose breadcrumbs.
6 Either fry separately in deep fat or cook in the fat surrounding the meat until golden and crisp.
7 Drain on kitchen paper.
8 Serve with the meat.

SAGE AND ONION STUFFING (pork, goose and duck)

1 large onion	Seasoning
50 g breadcrumbs	1 teasp. dried sage
25 g shredded suet	Beaten egg

1 Peel onion. Cut into quarters and cook in boiling salted water until tender.

2 Place breadcrumbs, suet, seasoning and sage in a basin. Mix.
3 Strain onion when cooked. Reserve 2 teasp. of liquid to mix with stuffing.
4 Chop onion finely. Add onion and stock to breadcrumb mixture. Mix well.
5 Bind together to a very stiff consistency with beaten egg.

HAM OR LIVER STUFFING (chicken)

100 g chicken or calves liver or ham (raw)
25 g margarine
50 g breadcrumbs
Seasoning
2 teasp. chopped parsley
½ teasp. mixed herbs
Grated zest ½ lemon
Beaten egg

1 Wipe over the meat. Finely chop up liver or ham.
2 Melt margarine in a small pan. Lightly fry meat in the pan until tender.
3 Remove pan from heat. Add all the dry ingredients. Mix well.
4 Bind together to a stiff consistency with beaten egg.

NUTS AND RAISIN STUFFING (meat or vegetables)

50 g breadcrumbs
25 g margarine
50 g seedless raisins
50 g chopped nuts
Seasoning
1 teasp. chopped parsley
Beaten egg

Follow recipe as for veal stuffing. Add nuts and raisins with the seasonings.

PRUNE STUFFING (chicken, veal, pork, duck)

6 large cooked prunes
1 small cooking apple
Pinch grated nutmeg
25 g chopped nuts
Seasoning
50 g breadcrumbs
Grated zest and juice ½ lemon
25 g shredded suet
Beaten egg

1 Stone the cooked prunes. Chop.
2 Peel the apple and grate.

3 Place all ingredients except the egg in a large basin. Mix well together.
4 Bind together with beaten egg to a stiff consistency.

APPLE AND CELERY

1 small onion   *25 g margarine*
25 g ham or luncheon meat   *50 g breadcrumbs*
(cooked)   *Seasoning*
2 sticks celery   *Beaten egg*
1 small cooking apple

1 Peel and chop onion finely. Chop ham or luncheon meat and celery. Grate apple.
2 Melt margarine in a small pan. Lightly fry chopped onion in the fat until tender, about 10 mins.
3 Remove pan from heat.
4 Add all ingredients except for the beaten egg to the ingredients in the pan. Mix well.
5 Bind together with a little beaten egg to a stiff consistency.

MUSHROOM (fish, meat or vegetables)

25 g bacon   *50 g breadcrumbs*
50 g mushrooms   *Seasoning*
25 g margarine   *Beaten egg*

1 Remove rind from bacon. Cut into very small pieces.
2 Wash, dry and chop mushrooms finely.
3 Melt margarine in a pan. Lightly fry bacon and mushrooms in the fat until tender.
4 Remove pan from heat. Add all other ingredients except for beaten egg. Mix well.
5 Bind together with beaten egg to a stiff consistency.

SHRIMP STUFFING (for white fish)

1 small onion   *Seasoning*
50 g peeled shrimps   *½ teasp. anchovy essence*
25 g margarine   *zest and juice ½ lemon*
50 g breadcrumbs   *Beaten egg*
1 teasp. chopped parsley

1 Peel and chop onion finely. Rinse shrimps to remove salt. Chop finely.
2 Melt margarine in a pan. Lightly fry onion in fat for 10 mins.
3 Remove pan from heat. Add all other ingredients, except beaten egg. Mix well.
4 Bind together with beaten egg to a stiff consistency.

CHESTNUT STUFFING (poultry or veal)

500 g chestnuts
250 ml stock
25 g margarine
¼ teasp. Marmite

Seasoning
Pinch cinnamon
½ teasp. sugar

1 Place chestnuts to boil in a pan of water for 10 mins. Shell and skin them a few at a time. Keep unshelled chestnuts in the water until you are ready for them.
2 Place shelled chestnuts back in the now empty pan. Add stock, stew until soft, 20–30 mins. Drain well, keep the stock.
3 Pass chestnuts through a wire sieve.
4 Melt margarine. Dissolve Marmite in a little of the stock.
5 Added melted margarine, Marmite, sugar and seasonings to the chestnuts. Mix well.
6 Mix to a slightly sticky mixture, using the stock.

SWEET CORN STUFFING (poultry, meat and fish)

1 small onion
1 small tin sweet corn
15 g margarine
Seasoning
25 g breadcrumbs

Grated zest and juice
½ lemon
Pinch grated nutmeg
1 teasp. chopped parsley

1 Peel and chop onion finely. Drain sweet corn.
2 Melt margarine, fry onion for 5 mins. Add sweet corn, fry for a further 5 mins.
3 Remove pan from heat. Add all other ingredients except for the egg. Mix well.
4 Bind together with beaten egg to a fairly stiff consistency.
5 Taste, add any further seasonings.

Dressings

WHITE SAUCE DRESSING

250 ml Béchamel sauce   Seasoning
(pouring) $\frac{1}{8}$ teasp. made mustard
15 g margarine $\frac{1}{4}$ teasp. sugar
1 egg yolk
2 tablesp. vinegar

1 Prepare Béchamel sauce. Turn off the heat.
2 Add margarine to the hot sauce. Stir well until margarine has melted.
3 Add egg yolk. Return to heat. Cook gently, stirring all the time without boiling. Taste. The sauce should now be slightly thicker.
4 Leave sauce to cool. Cover with wet greaseproof to prevent skin forming.
5 Gradually whisk in the vinegar and seasonings to the cooled sauce.
6 Serve in a sauce boat.

N.B. 1 teasp. chopped chives, mint, parsley and tarragon may be added to this sauce and used for a potato salad.

FRESH DRESSING

4 tablesp. olive or salad oil $\frac{1}{4}$ teasp. dry mustard
2 tablesp. vinegar or lemon   Seasoning
juice   A few drops Worcestershire
$\frac{1}{4}$ teasp. sugar   sauce

1 Place all ingredients into a screw top jar or bottle. Screw lid on tightly.
2 Shake ingredients vigorously until the oil forms an emulsion with the other ingredients. This is noted by a cloudy look on the mixture.
3 Serve dressing immediately. On keeping, the dressing separates out, but may be reshaken before use.

ENGLISH SALAD DRESSING

1 yolk, hard boiled egg   Seasoning
1 tablesp. olive oil $\frac{1}{8}$ teasp. made mustard
2 teasp. vinegar   2 tablesp. double cream or
1 teasp. Worcestershire sauce   evaporated milk

1 Sieve egg yolk into a basin.
2 Gradually add the oil, vinegar and seasonings. Work in well.
3 Whip cream or evaporated milk. Fold into the egg and oil mixture.
4 Serve with the salad or in a sauce boat.

YOGHURT DRESSING

1 carton plain yoghurt *¼ teasp. made mustard*
⅛ teasp. sugar *2–3 drops lemon juice*
Seasoning

1 Empty carton of yoghurt into a basin.
2 Add all other ingredients. Mix well.
3 Serve in a sauce boat.

EVAPORATED MILK DRESSING

2 tablesp. evaporated milk *Pinch dry mustard (to taste)*
1 tablesp. lemon juice *¼ teasp. sugar*
Seasoning

1 Place evaporated milk and half of the lemon juice into a basin. Whisk until thick and frothy.
2 Gradually work in the remaining ingredients. Mix well.
3 Serve in a sauce boat.

CONDENSED MILK DRESSING

2 tablesp. condensed milk *Seasoning*
2 tablesp. vinegar *Pinch dry mustard (to taste)*

Make as for evaporated milk dressing.

MAYONNAISE

1 egg yolk *2 shakes pepper*
125 ml olive oil *Few drops Worcestershire*
¼ teasp. dry mustard *sauce*
¼ teasp. salt *2 tablesp. vinegar or lemon juice*

1 See that the egg yolk and oil have been kept in a cool place for half-an-hour before use, but not in a refrigerator.
2 Place egg yolk in a basin. Add all seasonings, except vinegar or lemon juice, beat well with a wooden spoon or whisk.
3 Put the oil into a clean vinegar bottle with a sprinkler top.
4 Add the oil drop by drop to the egg mixture (beating well after the addition of each drop), until the mixture thickens.
5 At this stage the oil may be added in a continuous thin stream, beating all the time.
6 When the emulsion becomes too thick to beat, add the vinegar or lemon juice drop by drop in the same way as the oil. Repeat this process until all the oil and vinegar is used and the mayonnaise is as thick as double cream.
7 Taste, add any further seasoning if required.
8 Serve in a sauce boat.

N.B. If mayonnaise curdles, add drop by drop to another yolk and whisk well, using electric mixer if you have one.

BOILED SALAD DRESSING

15 g flour
1 teasp. sugar
1 teasp. salt
½ teasp. dry mustard

¼ teasp. pepper
1 egg yolk
125 ml milk
15 g butter

1 Place all dry ingredients in a basin. Mix well together.
2 Gradually add the egg yolk and milk, stirring all the time.
3 Place margarine in a basin.
4 Boil water in a pan. Place basin with margarine over the water until margarine melts.
5 Add egg and milk mixture to the melted margarine.
6 Stir the mixture continuously over the water until it thickens.
7 Remove from heat. Add vinegar—stirring. Cool—covering with damp greaseproof paper.
8 Serve cold in a sauce boat.

N.B. This dressing may be bottled when cold for future use.

VINAIGRETTE DRESSING

$\frac{1}{4}$ teasp. salt
4 tablesp. salad oil
2 tablesp. vinegar
1 teasp. chopped gherkins

1 teasp. chopped parsley
$\frac{1}{2}$ teasp. made mustard
$\frac{1}{4}$ teasp. pepper
1 teasp. chopped chives

1 Place all ingredients in a jar or bottle with a screw top, as for French dressing.
2 Shake until it appears cloudy, as for French dressing.
3 Serve and use at once.

20
Special diets:vegetarians, invalids and slimmers

(For further details reference may be made to specialist books)

Vegetarians

These fall into two classes:

(a) Vegans, who will eat no food from an animal source. Their diet is bulky, limited and monotonous. Care must be taken to ensure enough vegetable protein is served and vitamins A and D are given (enriched margarine). Cooking fats must be from vegetable sources.

(b) Lacto-vegetarians, who will eat eggs, milk and cheese but not meat and fish. Again care must be taken to provide sufficient protein, the egg, cheese and milk protein being supplemented by vegetable protein, and that some biteable foods are provided.

Suitable dishes (see other chapters) include: savoury flan, cheese flan, cheese pudding, macaroni cheese, cauliflower and eggs au gratin, omelettes, stuffed tomatoes (cheese), cheese straws.

EGG CROQUETTES

3 hard boiled eggs   *Egg and raspings for coating*
125 ml white panada sauce   *Parsley for garnish*
Seasoning

1 Chop eggs finely or sieve.
2 Make a panada roux sauce (see Sauces), with flour, margarine and milk.

3 Add the eggs to the sauce, season and mix well. Leave till cold. Divide into equal pieces.
4 On a floured table make into cork shapes. Coat twice in egg and raspings.
5 Fry in deep fat till golden, drain. Serve on an oval plate, garnished with parsley.

MACARONI A L'AMERICAINE

100 g macaroni   *Seasoning*
30 g margarine   *Pinch of sugar*
50 g plain flour   *Croûtons of fried bread*
400 ml tomato puree

1 Break up the macaroni. Cook till tender in boiling salted water (20 mins.).
2 Make a roux sauce with the margarine, flour and sieved tomato (see Sauces).
3 Add the macaroni, seasoning, sugar. Reheat.
4 Serve in an oval dish, garnished with croûtons.

TOMATOES AU GRATIN

500 g tomatoes   *Seasoning*
100 g grated cheese   *100 g breadcrumbs*
25 g margarine   *Parsley for garnish*

1 Oven 350°F/Gas Mark 4. Grease a pie dish.
2 Blanch, skin and slice tomatoes.
3 Put a layer of cheese and crumbs at the bottom of the dish. Follow with tomatoes, then cheese and breadcrumbs, seasoning each layer. Dot with margarine.
4 Bake for 15 mins. till golden brown. Garnish with parsley.

Invalids and Convalescents

Rules for serving and planning

1 Meals must be well balanced with plenty of protein and vitamins in order to build up the body and fight infection. Too much energy-giving food should be avoided.
2 Doctor's orders must be obeyed.
3 Meals should be regular and often.

4 Meals should be prepared with great attention to cleanliness, to prevent infection.
5 Meals should be served attractively. A well laid tray with pretty china and cloth, etc., helps to stimulate the appetite.
6 Do not overload the tray.
7 Leave cooling drinks always to hand.
8 Avoid serving foods which are too spicy or greasy or using indigestible methods of cooking.
9 Avoid cooking foods with strong smells, as these could penetrate the sick room.
10 Remove the tray and left-overs immediately.
11 During convalescence more substantial dishes may be introduced with larger portions and more energy-giving foods may be served.

Suitable dishes (see other chapters):
Egg nog, beef tea, lemon barley water, apple snow, baked egg custard, soufflé, steamed fish, steamed chop, milk pudding, fruit fool, milk shake, etc.

Slimmers

The aim is to lose weight and this can only be achieved by cutting down calorie intake. 1,000 kcals per day is a good guide. However, the diet should still include sufficient nutrients.

Starchy and sugary food ("empty calories") must be reduced to a minimum; sweeteners and bread substitutes may be used.

Fats should not be reduced too much, as these help to prevent hunger.

Intake of vegetables should be high to provide vitamins and help prevent hunger.

Variety is important or the diet will be broken because of its monotony. It is advisable to gain a doctor's advice before beginning a diet. With care, several of the recipes in this book may be adapted and used in a slimming diet, e.g. salads, protein dishes.

21

Preservation and convenience foods

Aims
1 To preserve food for out of season use.
2 To retain colour, flavour and nutritive value.
3 To arrest decay by inactivating the organisms which cause it, e.g. yeasts, moulds, bacteria, enzymes.
4 To avoid wastage when there is a glut and take advantage of low prices.

Principles
Jam making—increasing the sugar content and boiling.
Pickling—increasing the acid content and adding salt.
Drying—removing moisture.
Deep freezing—lowering the temperature which inactivates the decay causing organisms and bacteria.
Salting—increasing the salt content.
Bottling—boiling, increasing the sugar content and removing air.

LEMON CURD

4 medium or 3 large lemons   *100 g butter*
5 eggs   *500 g caster sugar*

1 Grate the zest finely. Place in a double saucepan or in a bowl over hot water. Add the juice, butter and sugar, and the eggs.
2 Heat gently (do not allow the water to boil), stirring until the mixture is thickened and coats the back of a spoon.
3 Pour into clean warm jars. Cover immediately with waxed paper. Label.

N.B. All yolks may be used, 2 yolks for each egg in the recipe. Yields approximately 1 kilo.

JAM

1½ kilos fruit   *1½ kilos granulated loaf sugar*

Water as follows:
To each 1½ kilos fruit:

Apricots 250 ml   *Blackberries 600 ml*
Blackberry and apple 250 ml   *Blackcurrant 1½ litres*
Plum 250 ml   *Raspberry, strawberry none*

1 Wash and prepare fruit (use just ripe, unbruised fruit).
2 Put the fruit into a preserving pan with water. Bring to the boil. Simmer gently till softened. Add the sugar. Heat gently till dissolved. Bring to the boil.
3 Boil rapidly until setting point is reached, approximately 20 mins., depending upon the fruit. To test for setting— the jam will flake off the spoon and a teasp. of jam placed on a plate will form a skin and wrinkle after 1–2 mins.
4 Pour into warm dry jars. Cover immediately or leave until cold, cover and label.

N.B. If the pectin content of the fruit is low (e.g. strawberries, rhubarb) and the jam will not set, add lemon juice or the commercial pectin preparation 'Certo'.
Yields approximately 2½ kilos.

MARMALADE

1½ kilos Seville oranges   *2½–3 litres water*
Juice of 2 lemons   *3 kilos sugar*

1 Scrub and pour boiling water over the fruit. Peel off the rind, removing any pith.
2 Chop or finely shred the peel according to taste.
3 Put the pith and pips in a muslin bag. Squeeze juice from the fruit.
4 Soak the peel and fruit in the water overnight.
5 Bring to the boil with the pips and peel in the muslin bag. Add juice of orange and lemons. Simmer till the peel is soft, then remove bag. Add the sugar.
6 Bring to the boil. Test for setting point as in jam. Pour into clean, dry jars, label. Cover. Yields approximately 5 kilos.

SPICED VINEGAR

25 g pickling spice or
5 g mace
5 g whole cloves } *to*   *1 litre vinegar*
10 g whole all-spice   *15 g cinnamon bark*

1 Place in a bowl over a pan of hot water. Cover with a plate.
2 Bring to the boil. Remove from the heat. Leave to stand for 2 hours, strain.

RED CABBAGE

1 kilo cabbage   *1 litre spiced vinegar*

1 Remove any bruised leaves. Shred the cabbage.
2 Place in a bowl in layers with salt. Leave 24 hours, drain, rinsing off excess salt.
3 Pack in bottles, cover with spiced vinegar and suitably airtight. Leave for about a week before using.

PICKLED ONIONS

1 Use small pickling onions. Place unpeeled in brine made from 4 litres water and 500 g salt.
2 Leave 12 hours, peel. Place in fresh brine, weight them below the surface and leave 24–36 hours.
3 Remove, drain well.
4 Pack into jars. Cover with cold spiced vinegar. Keep 3–4 months, before using. Not sealed.

PICKLED CAULIFLOWER

1 Break the cauliflower heads into small pieces. Place in a large bowl. Cover with brine (4 litres water to 1 kilo salt).
2 Stand 24 hours. Drain, place in jars.
3 Cover with spiced vinegar. Seal.

APPLE CHUTNEY

3 kilos cooking apples	*250 ml vinegar*
1 kilo onions	*15 g ground ginger*
250 ml water	*¼ teasp. pepper*
50 g salt	*1 kilo sugar*
15 g cinnamon	*500 g golden syrup*

1 Peel and core apples. Mince or chop finely with the onions. Simmer in the water for 20 mins.
2 Add the salt, spices and half the vinegar. Cook until softened.
3 Add sugar, syrup and the rest of the vinegar. Simmer until thickened. Pour into warm dry jars. Cover and label.
   Yields approximately 3 kilos.

GREEN TOMATO CHUTNEY

2 kilos green tomatoes	*12 red chillies*
500 g apples	*15 g salt*
500 g onions	*500 g brown sugar*
250 g raisins	*500 ml vinegar*
15 g dried whole ginger	

1 Chop the tomatoes. Peel, core and chop the apples. Chop onions and raisins.
2 Mince all fruit.
3 Bruise the ginger and chillies and tie in muslin.
4 Place all ingredients in a pan, bring to the boil, simmer till thick.
5 Remove the bag of spices. Pour into warm, dry jars. Cover, label.
   Yields approximately 3 kilos.

DRYING HERBS

e.g., parsley, mint, sage, thyme, rosemary, tarragon.
Gather young leaves when dry. Wash, tie in bundles.
Hang in a warm place or dry in a cool oven. Crush, bottle.

Deep freezing
All items to be sealed carefully and labelled with the date before freezing. Use in rotation.

SOFT FRUIT

Wash, prepare fruit according to kind. Remove excess water. Place the fruit individually on large trays and place in the deep freeze till frozen. (This prevents fruit from sticking together during freezing.) Remove from trays, place in polythene bags, or waxed cartons. Remove as much air as possible and seal. Replace in the freezer till required.

Alternative method is:

1 Prepare fruit.
2 Put with sugar in polythene bags in amounts that can be used in one go.
3 Freeze.

VEGETABLES

Prepare according to kind, blanch and drain carefully. Pack in bags or cartons. Exclude air, secure, freeze.

MEAT

Pack joints in polythene bags, foil or moisture-proof paper, seal, freeze.

Separate chops with pieces of foil. Pack as for joints.

HERBS

Mint and parsley. Wash, chop. Pack into small polythene packets, enough for one quantity of sauce. Freeze.

MADE UP DISHES

Pies—keep in dish, wrap in foil. Seal. Freeze.

Cakes—Remove from tins, cool. Wrap in foil or store in plastic container. Seal, freeze.

Stews, etc.—Place in waxed cartons. Seal. Freeze. Foil containers may also be used.

N.B. Care must be taken when adding seasonings, spices, flavourings, etc. as during freezing their strength increases.

Convenience foods

Care must be taken in the choice and use of convenience foods in order that the housewife should obtain as many advantages as possible, but that her craft and nutritional standards do not suffer.

Varieties of convenience foods available include: canned, dried, packaged, cake mixes, etc., frozen, accelerated freeze dried, etc.

Advantages of use

1 Quick and easy to use. Time and labour and sometimes fuel are saved.
2 There is no waste.
3 Foods out of season may be easily obtained, which adds variety and interest to the diet.
4 Some foods (especially A.F.D. or frozen vegetables) are light and compact to carry, which is helpful to the woman who works and shops at a distance from her home.

Disadvantages

1 Cost—they usually prove to be more expensive.
2 Food value: starch is generally high, there is often a lack of sufficient protein (especially in complete meals, meat pies, etc.) and vitamin C.
3 Meals entirely composed of convenience foods tend to be monotonous and lack bite and bulk.
4 Portions are generally small, insufficient to satisfy the stated number of people.
  To obtain the greatest advantage from convenience foods, combine with fresh as much as possible.

Menu examples:

BREAKFAST

Tinned grapefruit, frozen kipper fillets, grilled fresh tomatoes, toast and marmalade, coffee.

15—ACB • •

LUNCH

Tinned orange juice, fried fish (frozen, own batter), frozen chips and peas, parsley sauce (pkt. mix). Lemon meringue pie (filling plus a fresh lemon). Instant coffee.

HIGH TEA

Shrimp flan (pastry mix, tinned or frozen shrimps), salad. Fruit in jelly. (Tinned fruit, packet jelly.) Sponge cake (packet mix). Tea.

DINNER

Tomato soup (dried), steak and kidney pie (frozen pastry), frozen brussels sprouts, fresh carrots, creamed potatoes, gravy, fresh fruit salad, blancmange.

22
Uncooked cakes and sweets

CHOCOLATE KRACKOLATES

(a) *25 g margarine*
1 tablesp. syrup
1 level tablesp. cocoa

50–75 g cornflakes, Rice Krispies or Sugar Puffs

1 Put margarine and syrup in a pan, melt, do not boil.
2 Remove from heat, stir in cocoa.
3 Add enough cornflakes to use all the mixture. Pile into cases, leave to set.

(b) *100 g cooking chocolate*

50 g cornflakes or Rice Krispies or Sugar Puffs

1 Melt the chocolate in a basin over a saucepan of water (this water must not boil). If chocolate gets too hot or water is added it will be spoilt.
2 Remove from heat, stir in enough cornflakes to use up all the chocolate. Pile into cases. Leave to set.

MARSHMALLOW POPS

100 g of toffees (different flavours, e.g. mint, treacle, may be used to give different results).

100 g marshmallows
100 g margarine
200 g Rice Krispies

1 Melt the toffees, marshmallows and margarine, stirring, do not boil.
2 Take off heat and stir in Rice Krispies.
3 Press into a 15 cm square tin about $2\frac{1}{2}$ cm thick, leave to set, then divide into pieces and put in cake cases.

HONEY NUT CRUNCH

50 g chocolate
100 g margarine
50 g caster sugar
1 tablesp. honey

25 g rolled oats
25 g chopped almonds
50 g cornflakes

1 Cut chocolate into small pieces.
2 Put fat, sugar, honey into a saucepan, melt.
3 Add chocolate, boil until thick.
4 Stir in oats, almonds and cornflakes.
5 Pile into paper cases, leave to set.

COCONUT ICE

500 g icing sugar
100 g desiccated coconut
1 egg white

About 2 tablesp. condensed milk or fresh milk
Cochineal or red colouring

1 Sieve icing sugar, add coconut.
2 Slightly beat the egg white, add to the mixture with enough milk to make a stiff pliable consistency.
3 Knead 5 mins.
4 Divide into 2 pieces.
5 Colour half pink, knead through the mixture.
6 Shape the pieces into 2 oblongs and roll out on a table, lightly dredged with icing sugar. Equal oblongs about 1 cm thick are needed.
7 Pack closely together in a tin, lined with waxed paper. When firm, turn out, cut into squares, put in sweet cases.

PEPPERMINT CREAMS

1 egg white
250–350 g icing sugar

Peppermint essence or oil of peppermint

1 Whisk egg white slightly.
2 Sift in 250 g. icing sugar and beat till smooth with a wooden spoon.
3 Add more icing sugar until a pliable, non-cracking consistency is obtained.
(Do not make too dry.)
4 Add tip of a teasp. of essence and knead through the mixture. Taste and add more if needed.
5 Knead 5 mins., wrap in waxed paper, leave 30 mins.

6 Roll out on icing sugar to $\frac{1}{2}$ cm thick, cut with a $2\frac{1}{2}$ cm cutter.
7 Dry 24 hours on a flat dish, pack separately from other sweets.

UNCOOKED CHOCOLATE FUDGE

200 g plain chocolate   *2 level tablesp. condensed milk*
100 g butter or margarine   *1 teasp. vanilla essence*
1 egg beaten   *50 g chopped nuts (optional)*
500 g icing sugar

1 Melt chocolate and butter together over hot water.
2 Mix egg, condensed milk, essence together. Beat in blended chocolate and butter and icing sugar.
3 Stir in nuts, turn into a greased tin 15 cm square.
4 Chill in fridge several hours. Cut into pieces.

RUM TRUFFLES

100 g butter or margarine   *Rum to flavour*
100 g chocolate   *Chocolate vermicelli or drink-*
25 g icing sugar   *ing chocolate*

1 Cream butter, melt chocolate over hot water and add to butter. Stir in icing sugar and rum.
2 Form into small balls. Roll in vermicelli or drinking chocolate. Leave to set. Put in sweet cases. Cherries and cherry brandy may be used instead of rum. Nuts may be added or the truffles rolled in chopped nuts.

CHOCOLATE TRUFFLES (alternative recipe)

50 g chopped toasted almonds   *100 g icing sugar*
50 g margarine   *100 g chocolate*
2 teasp. cocoa   *Chocolate vermicelli*
$\frac{1}{2}$ teasp. vanilla essence or
1 tablesp. rum

1 Blanch nuts (bring to the boil in a pan of water, cool, remove brown skin). Chop finely.
2 Put on a baking sheet, and brown in a moderate oven, shaking occasionally.
3 Melt margarine in a saucepan, add cocoa and stir till dissolved.

4 Remove from heat.
5 Add vanilla essence or rum. Add nuts and enough icing sugar to make a mixture which can be rolled into balls.
6 Taste and correct flavouring.
7 Form into balls, coat with vermicelli. Put in sweet cases.

TRUFFLES

300 g digestive biscuits
50 g drinking chocolate
25 g desiccated coconut

50 g margarine
1 small tin condensed milk
Desiccated coconut for rolling out

1 Crush the biscuits into crumbs, either by placing between greaseproof paper and pressing with a rolling pin, or in a liquidizer.
2 Add the drinking chocolate and coconut.
3 Melt the margarine with the milk, add to the dry ingredients, mix and roll into balls.
4 Roll the balls in coconut. Place in sweet cases.

ALMOND PASTE SWEETS

150 g ground almonds
300 g sieved icing sugar
1 egg

Drops of almond essence
Colouring

1 Put almonds and sugar together.
2 Beat egg and add almond essence, add to almonds, etc. Knead to make a pliable consistency.
3 Colour some pieces green or pink and make into balls, sandwiches, whirls, fruits, stars, etc. or use to stuff dates.

ROSE HIP CREAMS

5 teasp. lemon juice
½ teasp. finely grated lemon zest
4 teasp. rose hip syrup

Few drops vanilla essence
50 g icing sugar
15 g crystallised rose petals or violets

1 Put lemon juice, zest, rose hip syrup, essence in a bowl.
2 Add icing sugar to make a stiff paste.

3 Roll into about 18 balls. Place a crystallised petal or violet on each.
4 Leave on a plate dusted with icing sugar, in a cool place to set.

N.B. These are very sweet.

SNOWBALLS

50 g margarine
100 g caster sugar
2 tablesp. condensed milk

4 tablesp. rolled oats
2 tablesp. drinking chocolate
4 tablesp. desiccated coconut for rolling

1 Melt the margarine, add sugar and milk very slowly (do not allow to boil). Remove from heat.
2 Add the dry ingredients, mix, form into balls and roll in coconut. Serve in paper cases.

Index

Girdle scones, 118
Goulash, 50
Grapefruit, 19
  grilled, 20
  mint, 20
  & orange cocktail, 19
Gravy, 199
Green tomato chutney, 223

Ham stuffing, 210
Hamburgers, 49
Herbs, to dry, 223
Herring
  baked & stuffed, 35
  soused, 35
Honey nut boats, 160
  crunch, 228
Horse-radish sauce, 207
Hot pot, 45
Huffkins, 148

Icing
  American frosting, 140
  cream variations, 140
  glacé, 137
  royal, 138

Jam
  basic, 221
  buns, 115
  puffs, 168
  roly poly, 92
  sauce, 204
  sponge, 94
  tart, 99
  tartlets, 156

Kebabs, 42
Kedgeree, 36

Lamb, 37
Leeks, boiled, 77

Lemon
  barley water, 178
  butterfly, 31
  cream icing, 140
  curd, 220
  meringue pie, 100
  sauce, 197, 201
  soufflé, 106
Lemonade, 178
Lentil soup, 25
Liver
  fried, 57
  risotto, 57
  savoury, 56
  stuffing, 210

Macaroni
  à l'américaine, 218
  cheese, 65
Mackerel
  baked & stuffed, 35
  soused, 35
Madeira cake, 128
Maids of honour, 158
Maître d'hôtel
  butter, 205
  sauce, 199
Manchester tart, 101
Mandarin tartlets, 158
Marmalade, 221
  sauce, 204
Marrow, stuffed, 85
Marshmallow pops, 227
Mayonnaise, 214
Meat
  croquettes, 111
  loaf, 49
  pasties, 111
  & potato pie, 52
  roast, 37
Melon, 20
Melting moments, 135
Milk
  condensed, dressing, 214

Yorkshire Pud.

4 oz fluid
1 egg
2 tablespoon floor.
Salt.

Yorkshire Pud.

1 egg
1/4 pint milk
2 tablespoons plai ho-s.

2 oz Suga. =